ADVANCED
STILLWATER
FLYFISHING

ADVANCED STILLWATER FLYFISHING

Chris Ogborne

David & Charles

For Angie

A DAVID & CHARLES BOOK
Copyright © Chris Ogborne 1993
First published 1993

Chris Ogborne has asserted his right to be identified as author of this work in accordance with the Copyright, Designs and Patents Act 1988.

A catalogue record for this book is available from the British Library.

ISBN 0 7153 9982 9

Typeset in 10½ on 12½ pt Janson Text Roman by Icon Graphic Services, Exeter
and printed in Great Britain by Redwood Press Ltd
for David & Charles
Brunel House Newton Abbot Devon

CONTENTS

Introduction

THE QUALITY AND CONTENT of any book on angling will inevitably reflect the thought, methods and opinions of one person, the writer. Fishing, thank goodness, is still a sport where nothing is fully definable. More often than not, the trout will have the final word and that is how it should be. If everything was clear-cut and rational, I suspect that there would be far less pleasure than we now derive from our hours on the water.

Having said that, however, I would equally claim that there is huge fun to be had from trying to outwit the fish, from taking an inordinate amount of time in preparing for each outing, and from ensuring that our tackle and flies are of the highest order. The ability to read the water and the weather conditions, and perhaps to attain a kind of 'sub-surface vision' is the mark of a true angler, and someone who invests a little of himself in his sport is far more likely to succeed than those with a lesser commitment.

For more than thirty years of my life I have been a totally committed fly fisherman. The sport occupies an immense part of my thoughts, both in and out of season, and is pursued with a fanaticism that may appear unseemly to some people. My uncle in Sweden, who first introduced me to the fly rod all those years ago, told me that I should try to think like a trout, and this one piece of advice had stood me in good stead in my angling career. I have studied the fish and their environment, and more particularly I have studied the things that they eat as a cornerstone of my philosophy and approach. The vast majority of the flies that I tie and fish are based, either loosely or directly, on items that fish eat at some time or other. If anything in angling is proven, it must surely be that this is the most effective way of getting to grips with the fish.

For me, the essence of flyfishing is that the fish should have more than a sporting chance. Indeed, fly fishermen seem at times to take a perverse pleasure from stacking the odds against themselves. We fish tiny, food-imitating flies on gossamer leaders, and in the most hazardous and snag-ridden places, just for the challenge of it. When heavy leaders would suffice we still use fine ones, and when large lures would catch we still tie on a small buzzer. For many years now I have been advocating the 'light line philosophy' as opposed to some of the more brutal lure-fishing tactics that tend to prevail on some reservoirs, as I genuinely believe that it is a more ethical and sporting way of fishing. It is a happy coincidence that, in the long run, it does catch more fish. For this reason I make no apology for the fact that lure fishing, with its attendant heavy gear and lead-head flies, has no place in this book. The title is, after all, 'advanced' flyfishing, and there is little that is advanced, or subtle, or difficult about trailing a 3in streamer behind a drifting boat. In my view a fly should be cast and presented rather than paid out on 50 or more yards of lead-core trolling line.

There is a long history of flyfishing in my family, and according to my mother I am at least a 'third generation fanatic'. Certainly I owe a great debt to my father, who first fired my enthusiasm for the sport. For much of my angling career he has been both mentor and companion, but beyond this he has also been a true friend, which is something that I treasure. What we have goes beyond a normal father/son relation-

Everything a small stillwater rainbow should be

ship, and it has reached this stage largely because of our shared empathy with the countryside in general and the Mendip Hills in particular. Many of the nuances of tactic and technique illustrated in this book have been developed with his help, and in doing so we have enriched many happy hours together.

Any talk of fundamentally 'new' tactics in flyfishing has to be viewed at least with some qualification, not to say scepticism. I firmly believe that very little in our sport is genuinely new, but rather that it is a natural process of evolution and in some cases rediscovery. Things that appear at first glance to be revolutionary, such as the modern vogue of fishing a team of stillwater dry flies, is in fact little more than a development of the loch style technique. True, it involves some radically different flies and takes full advantage of the low diameter monofilaments that have so changed our attitudes to leaders, but in essence it is not all that far removed from the old 'typical' loch style of fifty years ago.

'Advanced' flyfishing, and indeed everything in this book, is the result of my thirty years in the sport. Above all, it is a book that has been researched for the last ten years, during which time I have travelled literally all over the world to fish a variety of stillwaters. The tactics that have evolved have proved just as effective on the lakes of Finland as they have on the loughs of Ireland. The flies that have been used have fooled rainbows and browns in New Zealand, in Europe and, of course, in Britain.

My style of fishing, the light line approach as it is often called, is essentially about fishing flies that suggest or represent items in the trout's food chain. In some ways it is a revision of traditional methods, hopefully embracing the ethics and first principles of flyfishing, while it also seeks to develop 'new' variations on established themes. Like all things in fishing it is in a constant process of evolution, and opinions and attitudes are modified as the years go by. New developments in the tackle industry make life easier for us from time to time, but hopefully the fundamental principles remain largely unchanged. It is our interpretation of them, as true anglers, that really matters.

This book is about advanced stillwater flyfishing, and as such there are inevitably some assumptions that need to be made. There is little point, and even less space available, for me to discuss every item of tackle available on the market. I have assumed that any reader will be in possession of at least the basics in terms of kit, and that he or she will be a reasonably competent angler. The book will not teach you to cast 35yd instead of 30; what it will do is to show you how to fish your existing 30yd more effectively, with greater confidence and, I hope, with a greater degree of success.

Blagdon Lodge

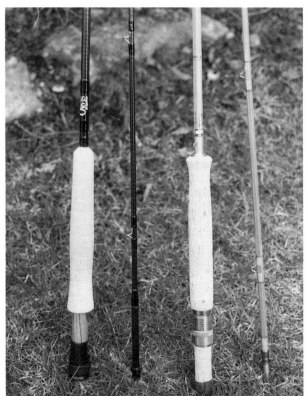

The old and the new: graphite and cane rods are products of great beauty, and both still have their place today

PART 1

TACKLE

This section of the book will not be over-long, as I have assumed that anyone reading about advanced flyfishing will already have a solid grounding in tackle knowledge. It is also an area of huge subjectivity and every angler will have his or her own opinion as to what constitutes an ideal outfit.

Anglers come in all shapes and sizes, and with varying levels of ability, and because of this each will have his or her requirements from the tackle that they use. In time, and provided that the outfit is essentially right for the individual in question, the rod will become an extension of the arm. As in shooting, you will only have to point the rod at the fish for the cast to be a good one.

In the last generation, and particularly in the last ten years, flyfishing tackle has taken some huge leaps forward. The transition from cane to glass to graphite has taken place in an incredibly short space of time, and the current fad of experimenting with different carbon mixes is largely a gimmick – the development of the carbon-fibre/graphite rod is arguable as good as it ever needs to be. Variations on the graphite theme are just that, as there are no significant advantages in the Boron or Kevlar mixes. Some of the claimed benefits are outweighed by major disadvantages, and most of the variations have more to do with marketing whim than with genuine product development.

Reels, too, have taken great leaps forward from the days when a brass reel could weigh pounds instead of ounces. It was just before the turn of the century that Hardy produced their first 'Perfect' reel, a model that in essence has barely changed since. Modern Perfects in alloy still retain the design principle of the original, with immaculate engineering that ensures that they will one day be collector's pieces, just as the early ones are today.

The development of most items of tackle has now reached the stage of fine-tuning, as opposed to radical innovation. Any product can be refined provided that you have sufficient budget, and those who are prepared to pay for the finest tackle will undoubtedly reap the benefits of it, if only in pride of ownership. With the degree of

The writer and Bob Church after a day's field testing of a new series of rods for Bob Church & Co

excellence currently available it is also folly to go for the cheapest items – in most cases they will wear our in a season or two, demanding expensive replacement. It is far better to extend your budget in the first place and to buy tackle that with care will last a lifetime.

True innovations are rare and in the field of fishing tackle they can be listed on the fingers of one hand. When they come they stand out clearly for what they are, making a positive contribution to the sport. Super-strong nylon monofilament and braided leaders are two obvious examples, both offering improved fly presentation, hooking properties and providing better balance to an outfit than was previously thought possible.

The debate on fly line development rambles on. For every paragraph extolling the virtues of non-stretch lines, you will read another to counter the argument. For me, the choice of fly line is almost as personal as the rod itself: some anglers will derive benefits from non-stretch lines, whereas others will be unable to use them.

Waterproof clothing has come a long way in a short time, and modern developments in fibre and fabric are significant. 'Breathable' garments are the clothing of the future and will undoubtedly spell the end for waxed cotton before too long. They are better wearing, more comfortable and a far better buy in the long term. I have never owned a waxed cotton jacket that did not leak within its first season, yet my current Musto jacket looks as good as new in its third year – and I am very hard on jackets. On warmer days my new Ventile jacket from Bob Church incorporates the vital properties of lightness in weight and complete waterproofing.

A soft-action rod is more sensitive to violent plunges by the fish

Then there is the seemingly endless list of extras, those hugely tempting items on display in every tackle shop across the land. We have all heard of, and no doubt many of us have been victims of, the term 'essential' tackle. If we believed everything that the manufacturers told us we would need a trailer to carry all our tackle around the fishery and a bank balance like that of an oil sheik.

Fortunately, everything that the manufacturers tell us is not necessarily true. You can survive happily with a minimal amount of gear, and all the gadgets in the world won't necessarily help you to catch more fish. For some strange reason there are still some anglers who think that by spending vast sums on a quality rod they will add around 5yd to their cast. The truth is that it may well improve their angling pleasure, but it will not necessarily make them into better anglers. The two things are fundamentally different.

What I propose to do, therefore, is to describe briefly the essential items of kit, largely as a preface to the much longer sections on technique and tactics. At the same time it will serve to explain a few of my idiosyncracies, which form a part of my angling style and which colour some of the specific tactics that I employ.

Rods

IT IS AN INESCAPABLE fact of life that 90 per cent of fly fishermen regard the rod as the most important single item of tackle. Obviously it is vital to the game, but I would suggest that there is an even more pressing case to settle upon the AFTM rating of your proposed outfit before you ever approach the rod counter in your tackle shop.

The AFTM rating is fundamental to the style of fishing that you will be undertaking and it will be crucial to the balance of the completed outfit. By definition, line weights of AFTM 8 and above cannot offer the subtlety of presentation needed for serious stillwater fishing, and the vast majority of top anglers will be using AFTM 7 or below. It is for this reason that I still suggest to newcomers and to those progressing in the sport that the first choice of tackle, well before rod and reel, is the fly line. With that choice goes a commitment to an angling philosophy that will govern both the success and pleasure of your fishing in the years that follow the purchase.

There is nothing 'purist' about choosing a lighter AFTM rating and neither does it necessarily restrict the user to a blinkered light line approach. Rather, it is that fishing outfits based on the 6 weight line, which mine are, will allow a huge range of tactics and techniques to be explored. The 6 line is light enough for subtle presentation, yet heavy enough to turn over a team of three flies at 30yd. It is powerful enough for prolonged distance casting without effort and to lift off 20yd of line when the occasion demands. Above all it has complete flexibility for all the types of fishing that are likely to be encountered, from the presentation of a tiny nymph through to the fast-stripped lure in a high wind.

I have assumed at this stage that anyone who is in the pursuit of excellence in fly-fishing will be aware of the fundamentals of rod design. They must also be aware of the advantages that a graphite rod holds over other materials: although it has not

A near-perfect ripple on Blagdon

entirely taken over from cane and glass, the benefits of graphite are obvious. Indeed, the current range available is superb, and I genuinely believe that the development of graphite as a material has now reached a stage of near-perfection. Most 'improvements' are primarily cosmetic and I see no real need for a rod that is lighter than what we have now or to try to change something that works so well. Graphite as a raw material does vary – there are many grades of quality. In most cases, the big name manufacturers are using high quality aerospace grade graphite as it is simply not in their interests to do otherwise. 'Back whipping' is strongly recommended in every case.

Specification

Obviously there will be a large element of personal choice here. Just as varying angling conditions require different rods, so too do the anglers themselves vary, in build, strength and ability. Having said that, there are still some specific requirements that can be identified in a stillwater fly rod, as well as some factors that need to be avoided. Not all the marketing hype that is put out by rod manufacturers is to be believed and it is not necessarily the most expensive rods that are the best. Because boat and bank anglers have different requirements from their rods, I propose to look at them separately.

BOAT RODS

The vogue for longer rods for boat fishing, which was largely a legacy from loch style generations past, has now passed. Modern graphite technology has provided us with shorter rods that will, in the main, out-perform those of ten years ago. The old school of thought that said that an 11- or even a 12-footer was needed is now long gone. In their place we have a modern trend towards a length of around 9½–10ft as being near 'ideal' for boat fishing. It is the perfect compromise length, blending all the subtlety of a short rod with the power and control of a longer tool. Personally, I still favour rods of 9ft 6in to 9ft 10in, choosing what would generally be termed a light action (middle to tip) and balanced to the AFTM 6 line. Most manufacturers will 'bracket' their line ratings for any particular rod, stating, for example, that it will handle lines in the 5 to 7 or in the 6 to 9 weights. In fact, the quality rods should be produced to handle one specific line weight, and it is less than fair to state that a rod will be 'comfortable' with weights of 5 to 9, as that range is too large. Even so, the flexibility of the modern product is such that it is fair to say that the rod will be capable of handling a line weight on either side of its actual specifications, which is why we see the range of three line weights quoted.

As will now be apparent, I base all my fishing on the AFTM 6 line weight. However, I will frequently use the same rods with an AFTM 5, particularly in calm conditions when presentation is vital. Conversely, these same rods will handle sinking lines, which are generally finer in diameter, in a 7 weight with no downturn in performance.

Modern loch style fishing, with all its variety, is a very 'active' fishing style. Very long rods are not easy to fish for a full day and they lack the precision for close-range work. Anything longer than 11ft cannot have the same degree of accuracy and presentation that can be achieved with a shorter rod, and for me a 12-footer makes too many physical demands on arms and wrists in a full day afloat.

The only caveat that I would issue here concerns the use of a long rod for exclusive styles. By this I mean that band of anglers who shun a really flexible approach to boat fishing and prefer to stick to the more traditional methods only. These anglers fish fast, short-line dibble techniques and restrict themselves to that style alone. For them, I fully accept that a long rod is more suitable and I wish them well with the method.

Similarly, it pays to have the option of a long rod in your armoury. There may well be days when you would like to experiment with dapping, or occasionally when you are obliged to go out in very tough conditions of big wind and wave. At such times, a longer rod can offer distinct advantages and the shorter tools become less than adequate. At all other times in the boats, though, which for me is about 90 per cent of my fishing, then the 9½ft AFTM 6 does everything I could wish of it.

BANK RODS

Stillwater bank anglers have a whole set of prerequisites for a fly rod, but nothing is more important than the ability to achieve good distance. Lake banks are popular places in summer and fish quickly learn that there is an 'exclusion zone' extending about 25yd from the margins. The fishermen who can consistently reach beyond this distance will unquestionably catch more fish.

Whilst distance is not everything, few would deny that it matters. In the past, many people resorted to the shooting head as a means of gaining those extra yards, but in most cases there was a severe sacrifice to make in terms of presentation: it is virtually impossible to get a clean turnover of the leader with a shooting head at anything over 20yd. A full fly line will always give better presentation, to the extent where it is worth sacrificing those extra yards in favour of a clean turnover.

Fortunately, there are many rods currently on the market that offer a good blend of power, distance and accuracy. The 'ideal' length for a distance rod is still a matter for personal choice, but it must be said that anything less than 9ft 6in is likely to be under-powered. A range of 9½–10½ ft rods is realistic, with a middle to fast-actioned 10-footer being the best compromise. This length is manageable and light enough for a full day's casting, while still retaining the necessary backbone for good distance.

It is a fact of life that most reservoir anglers think they are casting further than they actually are. In truth, few anglers can consistently reach beyond the 25yd mark and fewer still will regularly cast the full fly line. The 'average' caster will probably be presenting his flies at around 20–22yd, which is still a perfectly reasonable fishing range. However, with a properly balanced power outfit that same 'average' caster should be able to increase this to the magical 25yd mark without any sacrifice in presentation.

As ever in flyfishing, the word 'balance' is crucial. Contrary to popular belief, it is *not* necessary to use AFTM ratings of 9 or 10 to achieve distance. Provided that rod and line are matched and balanced, maximum range can be had with a power outfit based on AFTM 7 or even 6. In fact, some of the best professional casters in the world use AFTM 6, preferring it as the best all-round line weight.

Another myth that needs to be dispelled is that there is some fall-off in performance during a long casting session due to fatigue in the rod. This just does not happen, and the only 'fatigue' that is relevant here is on the part of the angler. Any rod will have a slight change in character due to temperature, but this is scarcely noticeable even by the most sensitive caster. Modern technology in graphite is such that some manufacturers are now able to offer a lifetime guarantee with their rods, which in itself speaks volumes. It is worth stressing, though, that the outfit needs to be suited to the caster – another aspect of balance: an angler of slight, slim build will not have the same requirements as a 16-stone trencherman. This is an obvious observation, yet all too frequently it is overlooked.

CUSTOM RODS

Any visitor to a modern tackle shop could be forgiven for thinking that anglers are spoiled for choice in terms of rod selection. At first glance the range appears baffling, with a myriad of lengths, styles and fittings. Again, modern technology is even able to offer us a whole range of coloured lacquers to choose from, allowing cosmetics to come into the equation.

Yet for some anglers even the best efforts of the manufacturers are not enough.

*Sage and Orvis rods. Different interpre-
tations on the quality theme*

*Grips and reel seats on some custom-
spec rods*

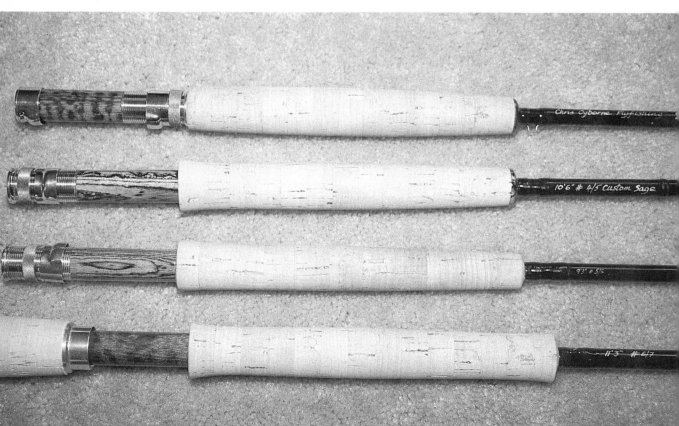

Either we don't like the colour, or the cork grip doesn't feel quite comfortable in our hand, or we would prefer a different wood for the reel seat. Someone once described top quality fishing tackle to me as being nothing more than 'male jewellery', and as an observation it is perhaps not too far wide of the mark. But in an age when so much is mass-produced, surely there is still room for a little individualism. There is much pride in ownership of a beautifully crafted custom rod, and while it will not necessarily improve your overall performance to any degree, it can still offer a lot of pleasure. If it feels better in the hand, then perhaps it will offer just that extra edge of confidence.

Rod Blanks

The first decision in this case will be the blank on which the rod is to be based, and all the comments made in the general rod section still apply here. Perhaps the biggest question of all will be whether to build the rod yourself, which requires some measure of ability and manual dexterity, or to entrust the job to an expert. There are many experts to choose from and your local tackle dealer will be able to advise you about the best one in your particular location. Most of the top quality makers will offer blanks as well as fully assembled rods, so there should be little problem in sourcing. After that, it is the actual fittings that need to be selected.

REEL SEATS/GRIPS

If the choice of the right fly rod for the individual angler is a personal one, then even more subjective must be the choice of fittings for that rod. In particular, the balance of the actual grip with the reel seat is an area where most anglers will hold conflicting views, and in the final analysis it all comes down to choice, which is as it should be.

Even so, there are some strong arguments for certain grip/reel seat combinations. Most reservoir rods up to 9½ft in length will have an up-locking reel seat: in other words, the reel is positioned close to the grip and about an inch or more from the bottom of the rod. This tends to give better balance when casting and is more comfortable for most single-handed casters. At this rod length, the choice of grip is wide, with cigar, scroll or half wells being the three principals.

Longer rod lengths will generally feature the full scroll handle, which offers a better hand grip to take the increased pressures when casting. They will also tend to have down-locking reel seats, again for balance, and may also feature a short extension butt. The latter is more for balance when playing a fish than for a casting aid. If you plan to use a heavier reel, then the down-locking seat should definitely be your choice.

My personal preference would almost always be a half-wells grip, with an up-locking seat. This fits in perfectly with my ideal rod length, at around 9½ft, although it is a good combination for all rods up to this length. I know that many distance casters will disagree, advocating the scroll grip, but I find that the added comfort of the half-wells actually adds to the general casting performance. With a custom-build rod, it is possible to have the grip 'cut' to the individual's hand, which provides the ultimate in comfort. This also serves to 'orientate' the grip in the hand and makes for supremely relaxed fishing.

ROD RINGS

One of the interesting things about flyfishing is the element of controversy that creeps into various discussions on tackle or tactics. Correspondence columns sometimes get taken over by heated debate, and I am always surprised at the way that gentle, placid anglers are capable of getting so worked up over such minor matters. In past years we have seen the 'battle of the fly line colours' – should they be light or dark? – and other arguments such as whether the booby nymph is legal, let alone ethical. Another great argument concerns rod rings, and here the tackle-makers have also had their say: are the best rings to be found in the new ceramic-lined guides, or are the traditional snake variety still the best? There are two schools of well-divided thought.

Just as I have to admit to favouring light-coloured floating lines, I also have to declare that I an totally in favour of the traditional snake rings. I find that they shoot the line further and more cleanly, and that they offer a better 'balance' to the rod.

Single-leg ceramic guides are, of course, easier to fix to the rod. They require only one lot of whipping (producing cost savings in the manufacturing process) and they are now virtualy the same price as stainless steel snakes. The problem with single-leg ceramics is that they have a tendency to pop out of their whippings, which is unfortunate if you happen to be in a big competition or are playing a fish at the time.

However, the advantages of good quality snakes are more fundamental than that, and it really boils down to friction: some ceramic guides actually have a large surface area in contact with the fly line, which adds to the friction. Stainless steel snakes offer less surface contact, with a correspondingly easier line shoot. Of course, quality is the most important factor as not all ceramics are the same. The cheaper varieties are useless, often with cracked liners or rough metal feet. The big name rod-makers use better rings, often back-whipping them for extra safety. Similarly, the latest generation of ceramics have smaller internal diameters, thereby solving the friction problem, and are now almost comparable to the snakes.

Snake rings also have their quality variants – poor ones are much worse than poor ceramics. The best are of the 'stand-off' variety as used by Orvis, Sage and the like, and these are superb. DIY rod-builders should always specify these, and your local tackle shop should be able to get them for you. If in doubt, the best rings are imported by a company called Hopkins & Holloway, and you can specify these to your dealer.

Badly applied rod rings can seriously damage your rod. Always use a fine file on the foot of the ring before whipping on, as any excess metal on the underside will dig into the graphite and could even cause a break. You should also follow the ringing instructions on the rod kit or blank and never be tempted to economise on rings by whipping on too few – bad spacing and under-ringing will spoil the performance of the finished rod. 'Back whipping' is strongly recommended in every case.

So much for the rods themselves. I will now discuss the choice of all the tackle to balance up the outfit. There are far too many 'essentials' on the market, and obviously manufacturers have a vested interest in convincing us that we just cannot afford to be without their latest creations. Care is needed therefore in the choice you make, so I have listed here only the items that genuinely fall into the essential category. But, I should also admit that I, too, have a weakness for new gadgets and gimmicks, and my tackle-bags are as full as anyone else's.

ROD TUBES

Modern fly rods are an expensive investment and it makes good sense to take out an insurance policy for them. Some people include them on their general household insurance, but the best and most effective way is to use some 'preventative' insurance and buy a decent rod tube.

Like most items of trout tackle these days, anglers are spoilt for choice when it comes to buying a rod tube. Many of the top makes like Orvis and Sage will actually come complete with a good quality aluminium tube, or they will at least have one as an option. But if your chosen rod simply comes in a cloth bag, the additional purchase of a strong carrying tube will be one of the best investments you can make.

There are some things to watch out for here. First, make sure that the tube is of good quality, thick gauge aluminium. Some tubes use too thin a wall of metal, and these are far too vulnerable. Any small dent will badly weaken the tube wall and can subsequently damage the rod inside. Expect to pay around £20 for a good quality tube. You will also need to make sure that the closure is a good one. The best ones are usually in brass, with a screw cap. You should allow at least 1in of space inside the tube, between the top of the rod bag and the screw closure.

For those who travel extensively, it is possible to buy aluminium tubes that will carry two or more rods. This makes good sense, as you then have the combined strength of all the rods as extra insurance. Various sleeves are available to cover the aluminium, with Cordura being the best: this is a type of heavy-duty canvas that is not only strong but also pleasant to handle.

If you have more than three rods to carry, you might consider one of the telescopic plastic carriers. these are strongly reinforced and will withstand anything that even the worst airline baggage-handlers can do to them.

Finally, and for the ultimate luxury in rod tubes, there are the leather cases. Lined in aluminium, such cases are real works of art and are a joy to own. They are a long way off being termed as essential, but for those who simply must have the best they are hard to beat. Unlike the bare aluminium tubes, which can get scratched and marked as time goes by, the leather tubes actually seem to look better with a bit of wear and tear.

Luxury extras: leather rod tubes and reel cases

Top quality fly reels from Ari Hart, Loop, and Orvis

Fly Reels

SOMEBODY ONCE SAID THAT the purpose of a fly reel was nothing more than to act as a storage reservoir for the fly line. While this has some truth, it takes absolutely no account of the many other factors involved, and certainly does not allow for the genuine pleasure that is to be had from using a finely engineered reel.

Modern fly reels are many and varied. Prices range from a few to many hundreds of pounds, with the finest reels being crafted from solid bar-stock alloy, with a custom hand-finish. They are very beautiful and are lovely to use, but they won't necessarily catch you any more fish. Indeed, when you are buying an outfit, one area in which considerable savings can be made is with the reel. As long as it is solid and mechanically reliable, it will serve you well and is is perfectly possible to buy such a reel for £20 or less. The development of modern materials has led to many advances in reel manufacture, and there are some superb reels on the market in Hi-tech plastic that are actually better than their metal counterparts. Such a reel is the Bob Church Lineshooter. This is an ultra-lightweight reel, which is well made and very well finished. Early models were in a pleasant olive-green colour, but later reels are a shade darker, blending better with most carbon rods. The reel has a wide diameter, which is a distinct advantage as it means that the line is stored in wider coils, thereby eliminating some degree of line memory. It offers superb control when playing a fish and the mechanics are totally sound.

Among the metal reels, there are several good value reels in the middle market. Rimflys have been around for a long time, as have the Pfluegers, and these are solid and reliable. They both offer interchangeable spare spools, which drastically reduces the price of an outfit, particularly for regular anglers who need to carry three or four densities of fly line with them.

Further up-market there is the excellent range of System Two reels, which feature a meaningful drag system along with finger control on the spool. At higher prices still there are the superbly engineered Hardy, Loop, Orvis or Ari Hart reels, designed and built to last a lifetime. In time, many will become either family heirlooms or even very expensive collectors' pieces.

The choice between metal and plastic is therefore largely subjective and is more likely to be influenced by budget than by anything else. The less expensive plastic or graphite reels are perfectly serviceable and will perform well. Yet there will always be a market for the more traditionally engineered metal reels, as anglers prefer the more solid feel and the metallic sound of the clicking pawls.

The only really crucial factor in your choice of reel is weight, coupled with balance. A very lightweight reel may feel unbalanced on a longer rod, or alternatively a heavy reel (like the Ari Hart) might be too heavy for a short light-line outfit. It is a matter of personal choice, but it should also be borne in mind that any outfit should be totally balanced and not just purchased in matching AFTM numbers.

Fly Lines

ONE OF THE IRONIES of fishing is that so many anglers are prepared to spend vast sums of money on beautifully matched rods and reels, yet those same people still penny-pinch when it comes to the equally important area of lines and leaders. I have actually seen someone in a tackle shop spend an hour over the selection of a rod and reel, pay well over £300 for the combination, and then ask the staff if they stocked mill-end lines! In terms of false economy, there can be nothing worse.

In the overall scheme of fishing, fly lines are relatively inexpensive. I say this in full awareness of the fact that some lines can now cost well over £40, and also that there will be some fishermen who violently disagree with the statement. The fly line is vitally important to our fishing, in some ways even more so than the rod itself, and it is sheer folly to try to cut any corners on grounds of cost.

As recently as twenty years ago the UK tackle trade was very conservative. Recently, though, and especially within the last ten years, modern technology has brought a new dimension to the business. The trade is now progressive, forward thinking, and more than prepared to embrace a rapidly growing band of stillwater flyfishing addicts. In just one generation it has undergone a revolution that has changed it irrevocably, and for the better.

Not surprisingly, the fly line is an item of tackle that has drawn most benefit from the modern approach. Hi-tech plastics now feature strongly in our everyday lives, and they are also an integral part of today's fly lines. In general, they are more supple yet more durable than they were, but probably the greatest innovation concerns the low- or non-stretch lines. In fact, there is nothing truly 'new' here, as the old silk lines were very low stretch in their day – something that tends to be overlooked in the current hot debates over 'normal' versus low-stretch PVC lines.

There are eloquent arguments on both sides of this particular table. The advocates of low-stretch lines will argue, correctly, that you have greater sensitivity and therefore more contact with things that are happening at the business end of the line. Those who prefer stretchy lines will say that they need a little 'give' to cushion the point of contact with the fish, or that they are more comfortable to cast. As always in matters where personal choice is offered, there can be no hard and fast rules. Personally, I find advantages in both low- and non-stretch lines, and while I have a distinct preference for low-stretch lines in all my sinkers, I still find that there are occasions when I like a degree of stretch in a floater.

What is beyond doubt, however, is that the overall quality of lines has risen dramatically in recent years, both in terms of the plastic coatings used and in the core materials. Those of us who fish hard and regularly – which in some cases means upwards of four times a week – formerly had to be prepared to buy at least two floaters in any season. Nowadays, it is possible that a good quality floater will last for a full season, and this includes some winter fishing as well – such is progress.

Again, there is a point here on economy: is just not worth trying to over-extend the life of any fly line. While in theory this is possible with the use of replasticisers and the like, in reality there is a marked fall-off in the performance of the line. In extreme cases a cracked line will quickly ruin the rod rings, but before that happens you will see a reduction in achievable casting distance, coupled with a slightly 'tired' feel to the line. Cleaning regularly will prolong the line's life, but in truth it is only delaying the inevitable: it is far better to buy a new one.

Three things are of fundamental importance to fly line selection, apart from the absolute basics such as the choice between stretch, non-stretch and quality. The first is the AFTM rating, which has been discussed comprehensively already in the section on rods. Then there is the choice of line profile, or taper, which primarily centres upon the DT (double taper) or WF (weight forward) alternatives. Finally, and perhaps most important of all, is the colour. These two factors need to be examined in some detail.

LINE PROFILE

The line profile is of secondary importance to its AFTM rating, but it is still very relevant. Again, modern technology has given us beautifully made lines in a whole range of tapers and formats to the extent where we are spoiled for choice, not to say confused. By far the best choice for distance casting, and indeed for all casting, is the weight forward or forward taper. Traditionally, these lines have contained most of the weight in the front 10yd of their length, but in recent years manufacturers have progressed the choice into further variations on the theme. The so-called 'rocket tapers' push even more weight into the front 5yd, but better still are the extended-taper WF lines. These work on the principle that many casters like to aerialise more than the obligatory 10yd, often having as much as 15yd in the air on a regular basis, before the final cast is made.

All of my lines are in WF format. I used to keep a few DT lines in reserve, primarily for river fishing, but this is no longer necessary. The WF lines work perfectly well on the rivers, and my casting style has now firmly modelled itself on this taper. When boat fishing, or indeed for any fishing situation, you should work towards using an absolute minimum of false-casts. The WF taper helps greatly in this respect, as do the super-slick finishes on most modern lines. With practice it is perfectly feasible to cast a full line with only one directional false cast. For good loch style, this is more or less compulsory.

There was once a theory that the WF format was only used where distance casting was a prerequisite, but this myth needs to be dispelled. Distance casting centres on one factor alone – the ability of the caster. A relaxed double haul will achieve the same distance, irrespective of line taper, and it can be achieved with such a laid-back rhythm that there appears to be no effort at all in the process. By contrast, there are others who work furiously at the false-casts, both arms at full stretch, and who appear physically exhausted after ten minutes. These are extremes, of course, but if you are in any doubt about your technique, there is no substitute for professional tuition. A few hours with a qualified expert are worth many years of practice.

Early season quality, at Bristol Reservoirs

LINE COLOURS

The best line colour for a floating line is an age-old bone of contention, and a subject that provokes some of the most heated arguments you will ever hear in angling circles. Some swear by darker colours like green or mahogany, whereas others will be adamant that the light colours are best, with white being first choice. There is even a small band of anglers who demand high-visibility orange, although I suspect that this has more to do with their eyesight than with anything else.

It is time to stand up and be counted, so I will declare here and now that I subscribe to the light colours. There are many reasons for this, not the least of which is to turn to nature itself: the bellies of most fish-eating birds like grebes and goosanders are white, and if it is good enough for them it is good enough for me. But beyond that, it stands to reason that a lighter colour will stand out less strongly against the predominantly light background of the sky. If you couple this with an element of visibility for the angler, who needs to be able to see the slightest movement at the end of his line and leader, there is a strong case for the colour white.

Darker colours are bound to stand out more against a light sky background. They are good for sub-surface lines, and in sinkers they are essential, with soft greys, greens and browns blending in well with the underwater environment. But for floaters I think they are a liability – they are simply much too visible at the surface. The high-visibility fluorescent pinks and oranges are even worse – I have actually seen fish boil away in fright as one of these lands on the water.

One of the best lines I have used in recent years is the Airflo glass floater, which is made in a clear transparent finish, with a very light green colour to it. This virtually disappears in the water, becoming all but invisible. A very strong argument can be made for a totally clear floating line, but as yet this is not available.

Line scare is another factor in this equation, and it relates directly to line colour. Excessive false-casting will inevitably show the line to the fish, and this problem is compounded if the bright fluorescent colours are being used. Lines that are excessively shiny will reflect a lot of sunlight, so caution is needed: reduce your false casting as much as possible, particularly from the boats.

Leader Materials

'TERMINAL TACKLE' IS THE collective name given to that mysterious commodity at the business end of the fly line. The leader is the final link between you and the fish, and if you do the job properly he should never see it. Modern technology is a significant factor here, and there have been some true innovations that have actually changed the way in which we fish: braided leader is one, but even more important is super-strength monofilament.

I am always surprised when tackle companies try to baffle their customers by talking about hi-tech equipment. After all, who knows anything about co-polymers, extrusion or other such wonders? So rather than giving you technical information I will simply say that the new monofilaments are effectively twice the strength for any given diameter. This means that you can either fish the same diameters that you used to and enjoy the extra strength, or alternatively you can use a much finer mono and still have the same breaking strain.

It all adds up to a huge benefit to the angler. With ever-increasing pressure on all fisheries, fish are becoming much more educated and line shy, and finer lines are a great help in catching them. Certain styles of fishing also demand a light line approach, non more so that the use of stillwater dries, and there are further advantages in this direction. Above all, it is in the presentation of the fly that super-strength nylons will score, as they give better turn-over as well as being less visible.

There is a price to pay for these advantages, and it comes in two forms. The first is price – these monofilaments are expensive, considerably more so than standard mono. However, when viewed against the overall cost of fishing, the price is relatively low and one that most fishermen are prepared to pay. The other disadvantage is the shine that is left on the material itself, which is simply due to the nature of the manufacturing process. It means that you need to pay close attention to leader treatment, taking as much of the shine away before use. Too much shine and the flash will scare fish, as well as making it difficult for your leader to penetrate the surface film. In this respect, there is a difference between the brands on the market, as some have a better colour than others and markedly less shine. Personally, I dislike the 'hard' colours and feel that the best materials are those with a totally neutral shade – in other words, no colour at all. The best are Orvis Super Strong, Tectan and the very new Loop brands.

There is also a variance in the suppleness of the brands. For example, both Drennan and Water Queen are relatively stiff, whereas Orvis is definitely on the supple side. I use Orvis for most of my leaders, but there are times when I prefer a stiffer mono like Loop, particularly in a big wind.

It should also be remembered that there are times when all the advantages of super-strength lines are negated. In dirty or murky water, for instance, or in really heavy algae blooms, there is no requirement for ultra-fine leaders and standard mono is actually better. For sinking-line work I am happy to use 'conventional' mono filament, as it has marginally better knot strength and is a fraction more secure.

That last point is worth explaining and it can be done by a simple analogy. A mountaineer or climber could use much thinner rope than he does, as most are immensely strong nylons. The reason that he does not is that the ropes tend to fray with use and become worn at the edge. Because of their thickness, however, they are still totally secure. The principle here is exactly the same.

Security of the leader is another area that needs comment, as you will have to take great care with your knots when you use super-strength. The old double blood knot is fine for standard mono, but is definitely not suited to these. Instead, use either grinner or water knots for leader construction, and tucked half-blood for attaching the fly.

There can be little argument that the super-strength, low-diameter nylons have had a tremendous effect on flyfishing. When used in conjunction with a light-line angling philosophy, which means a light and balanced outfit, they will undoubtedly improve your catch rate. They are obviously less visible to the fish, but even above this it is the improvements in presentation that win the day.

LEADER DISPENSERS

The latest newcomer to the fold of the super-strong nylons is the Loop brand. It sits in the middle ground in the suppleness/stiffness equation and provided that you use water knots to make your leaders, it has brilliant knot strength. It differs from all the other nylon lines primarily in the way in which it is presented: it comes on a neat 35yd spool that can be used on its own, but is really designed to be used with one of the best innovations I have seen for some time – a four-spool leader dispenser.

This remarkably clever system allows you to store four spools in one unit, all of different breaking strains. The spools are colour coded so there is no danger of using the wrong BS, and interchanging them could not be simpler. Once you have purchased the dispenser you simply order refill spools as you need them. The dispenser itself is very strong and beautifully engineered in lightweight plastic. It fits into any waistcoat pocket and is totally convenient.

Most important of all, it stores your leader material safely, free from all the knocks and bumps that tend to damage other leader spools in your pockets. Some dispensers are a problem because you cannot see when the line is running out, but not so with the Loop. The clear plastic means that everything is completely visible, and you can see at a glance when a spool needs replacing.

There are other dispensers on the market, but none compare with the Loop system. They are either too bulky, wrongly shaped or too fragile. Some are ridiculously fussy in their construction, completely negating the one factor that they are trying to promote – convenience.

Tackle-bags

IF ANYONE IN THE family is in any doubt as to what to give the fisherman in their life for Christmas, the two choices that always seem to win are either a fly-box or a tackle-bag. Fishermen can never seem to get enough of either and they are seldom wasted – after all, don't most of us possess enough tackle and flies to last at least two angling lifetimes?

Until recently, I was a devotee of the canvas tackle-bag. They look so good, and it seems that they have a tradition of their own, with that lovely leather trim and solid brass fittings. I still have my very first Brady bag, and although it looks rather tatty these days, I wouldn't dream of parting with it.

Canvas bags do have the disadvantage that they are not waterproof. On a wet day, especially in the bottom of a boat, they get well and truly soaked, as does everything inside them. It is largely for this reason that I changed allegiance a few years ago to some superb new bags from Wychwood tackle.

Wychwood was the brainchild of two people, one of whom I know very well, Dennis Moss. Dennis is a well-respected angler on the circuit, and he devised a totally waterproof range of bags that have retained all the good looks of the traditional tan-coloured canvas ones. They are dark green in colour, with strong nylon webbing reinforcements on all the seams, and have excellent webbing carrying straps.

My favourite bag in the range is the 'Boatman'. It is sufficiently big to take everything I need for a day afloat, with capacity for reels and spools, packed lunch,
fly-boxes, and even a light jacket. The interior is fully lined in a rubber material,
while the outside is in heavy-duty canvas. There are plenty of interior pockets for
spools or nylon, while the two main exterior pockets swallow up every fly-box
that I possess.

On a recent trip to Scotland, the Boatman bag passed what must be the ultimate
test for the product – airline baggage-handlers. I had a twinge of anxiety as I con-
signed all my precious gear at the check-in desk, but I need not have worried. It all
came out at the other end completely unscathed – the bag had provided complete
protection.

The Wychwood range has a bag for everyone, from a small shoulder-bag through
to the Boatman. The quality is consistent right through the range, and they are without doubt the best on the market.

Fly-boxes

FEW THINGS ARE MORE personal in fishing than a fly rod, but without any doubt the
fly-box is one of them. Anglers have very strong and fixed ideas as to what constitutes
the ideal fly-box, and these can range from something that looks like a miniature tea-
chest through to boxes smaller than a book of matches. The choice is endless.

With a subject as personal as this, it would be a braver man than me to offer advice.
However, there are certain things that the best fly-boxes will have in common, and
these are certainly worth considering before making a purchase.

First, the flies must be held securely so that they don't blow all over the place when
the box is opened. This is why the old traditional style boxes all had clips or compartments, even though the former can lead to rust problems and a consequent
weakening of the hook. For real security, I feel that the foam-lined boxes are ideal:
these are available with either flat foam sheet, or a ripple foam which is designed for
dry flies or hackled patterns – the ripple effect keeps the hackles and fibres from
becoming compressed.

The other main prerequisite is that your collection should be clearly visible, if possible in an orderly fashion. You will find that as your fly collection grows you will
need to segregate nymphs, attractors, dries and wets so that each can be clearly and
quickly identified. The Wheatley swing-leaf boxes are great in this respect, as you
have four leaves which can form the four main categories.

The best dry-fly boxes are still the ones with little spring-lid compartments, even if
they are a little more expensive. These are now available with foam on one side and
compartments on the other – a very workable compromise. Remember that dry fly
hackles will be ruined if they are crushed or compressed.

Finally, I also like to have one small 'black box' with me, which contains only the top
flies of the moment. This is very useful in competitions, where you need to be able to
identify the best flies on practice days and have them clearly presented on match day.
Apart from that, fly-boxes represent the ultimate 'personal choice' in angling.

A wide selection of palmered flies in a Wheatley clip box

The Ultimate Drogue

AN ESSENTIAL ITEM FOR the stillwater boat angler is a good drogue. On rough days it can be the difference between catching fish and being driven along unmercifully by the wind. It can turn unfishable conditions into a productive day and render even the worst weather quite bearable. Even on softer days, it provides a degree of fly control that can be vital, enabling the angler to explore the depths in a way that would be impossible in a free drift.

For such an item, one that is in great demand by almost every boat angler in the country, you might assume that fishermen would be spoiled for choice by the manufacturers. However, there are precious few commercially made drogues that come anywhere near to being right, and these are unnecessarily expensive and hard to find. It seems that British tackle-makers have a blind spot when it comes to drogues.

To be fair, one or two tackle-makers do get it right, the most notable among them being Bob Church, who markets an excellent and very serviceable drogue. All you have to do is to find a local tackle shop that stocks it!

However, for me and for most other thinking anglers, the only answer was to make our own drogues. This I set about doing, one rainy holiday day in Cornwall, many years ago. We were quietly browsing through the chandlery store, more to get out of the rain than with any real intent, when I glanced at the rows of galvanised shackles on the wall. Alongside them were the many gauges of rope that sea-going people

Drifting a good wave at Wimbleball – Drogue conditions

need, and as I looked at them together I began to form an idea about making my own drogue.

First, a drogue rope needs to be thick so that you don't cut your hands when retrieving it in a big wind. It also needs to be long, at least 15–18ft so that it sets at a reasonable depth behind the boat.

Then it needs to swivel, and here's where the shackle and swivel come in. In fact, these items serve a double purpose because, being quite heavy, they take the drogue down to an operating depth almost immediately. No longer do I have to mess about getting all the air out of the drogue: I simply throw it over the back, and the weight of the shackle and swivel does the rest.

You can attach a short length of chain to the shackle, but I find that this gives a bit too much weight. It is also rather cumbersome to carry around and there is more than enough weight in my fishing-bag as it is.

The 'parachute' part of the drogue is simply a square of canvas with a hole in the middle and four eyelets at each corner. You can either buy this ready made or construct your own with the help of a chandler.

And that's it! A strong, serviceable and totally reliable drogue that has never let me down. It folds up into a pouch (actually, the inside waterproof pocket of an old Barbour jacket) and this in turn sits at the bottom of my fishing-bag. The total cost, excluding the pouch, was about £9.

. . . .

32

Nets

EVERY ANGLER HAS HIS own idea of what constitutes the 'ideal' net, and some people are so fanatical about it that they even go to the extreme of making their own. It is a delicate subject indeed. Many of the landing nets in use today have more to do with tradition than with practical design. A belt-clip net might be good for the trout streams of the moors, but it has little place on our reservoirs: it falls down in terms of shape, capacity and ease of operation.

Nets are not cheap, so it pays to give some thought to their purchase. What shape is the best and how big should it be? What sort of handle do you need and what about its floatability? Do you need a separate net for boat fishing or is it possible to buy one that doubles up as a boat *and* bank net? Each of these questions needs to be considered in turn:

Shape Landing nets come in a variety of shapes ranging from teardrop to circular, oval and triangular. Given that most stillwaters can occasionally produce a big fish, the best choice is triangular. With this, you can easily see when the fish is well over the net before lifting him out – it's a clearly defined line. Bank anglers need their nets to double as line trays, which is the only practical shape for the purpose.

Capacity This is about a balance of 'normal' capacity, set against the occasional need for a big-fish net. For most stillwaters, a diameter of 20in should be regarded as a minimum, with the 'bag' being at least another 20in.

Handle This should be an absolute minimum of 36in in length, preferably nearer to 48in. The longer handle is useful where there are high banks to fish from, particularly on concrete banks or dam walls. A longer net will also sit nicely across the boat thwarts.

Construction Above all, the net should be light, making it easy to carry and manipulate. Better still, it should float as there will inevitably be occasions when you don't secure it properly on the bank or drop it overboard from the boat. The best materials are therefore of glass fibre, with a hollow but very strong shaft and arms.

Is there such a thing as the 'ideal' net that meets all these requirements and is suitable for both boat and bank fishing? Fortunately, the answer is yes, and the product is the Bob Church boat/bank net. This has been on the market for just a few years, yet it is already used by most of the serious competition anglers on the circuit. It is immensely strong, yet weighs only a few ounces. The shaft length is ideal and when folded – the arms slide down the shaft by means of a quick-release clip – it will fit into any car boot. It is perfect in the boats, is ideal on the bank and it still costs less than £25.

Braided Leaders

BRAIDED LEADERS, OR BRAIDED butt section leaders, are one of the most significant tackle developments of the last generation. This might seem to be a sweeping statement, but I am confident that it is true: this simple product has made such a radical difference to my own fishing that I rate it in almost equal importance with the advent of carbon fibre as a rod-building material. It really is that special.

Until as recently as ten years ago, braided leaders were unheard of. Like most new products they were first viewed with suspicion, then grudging acceptance, and finally now with praise. They were even unnecessarily banned at international competitions, but this rule has now been rescinded.

The basic function of a braided leader is to give clean turnover of the leader, with vastly improved presentation. It does this by transmitting the power of an unfurling fly line into the leader section itself. This smooth transition gives progressive turnover of the leader, and as a consequence the flies land cleanly on the water, in a straight line. Most good quality braided leaders are tapered, with the thicker end being joined to the fly line and the thinner end tapering to the tippet.

New technology has meant that we now have many alternatives from which to choose. There are simple braided butt sections, at about 3ft in length, for those who prefer to construct their own mono leaders. Then there are the full-length braided leaders, which come with the mono sections pre-tied and joined. They are available in pre-weighted form, with everything from floating format through to intermediate, sinking and fast sinking, thus enabling them to be precisely matched to the fly line in use.

It is impossible not to mention brand names here. The Orvis braided butts are ideal for those wanting a simple butt section. Bob Church also has an excellent range, but for the greatest variety it is hard to beat the Airflo system. This is available in everything from an individual leader through to an entire leader system for every kind of fishing you are likely to encounter in a lifetime in the sport. They have a simple loop-join system, which allows them to be quickly and easily interchanged as fishing conditions change during the day.

The latest developments in sinking leaders are particularly exciting. When used in conjunction with a sinking line of comparable density, they will quickly take your fly to the correct fishing depth – far faster than would previously have been possible. Again, the huge advantages in presentation are obvious.

With such major advantages, few anglers can afford to ignore braided leaders. They are inexpensive and easy to use, yet their effect on your fishing will be as marked as a change from glass to carbon in the rod itself.

. . . .

Opposite top left: *A good deep net ensures safety*

Opposite top right: *The author using the landing net as a line tray*

The long-handled nets provided by some fisheries, however, are less than practical. The shaft is heavy and cumbersome: it is far better to use your own lightweight net, which should float if the worst happens!

. . . .

Sundries

FLOATANTS

When I first started flyfishing, well over thirty years ago, there was only one floatant on the market. Called Mucilin, it was used for just about everything. Flies, leaders and fly lines were all treated with it, with little or no thought involved in the process. Like most other aspects of flyfishing in those days, it was very unscientific. Since then, modern technology has come to our aid. The industry that gave us carbon, boron, pearly tinsel and so many other wonderful things has also given us a new range of tackle preparations, and the development of truly excellent floatants are highly significant.

Fly fishermen as a body are conservative, so it is surprising that one of the newest products has become an instant and firm favourite – Gink. This is undoubtedly the best fly floatant that I have ever used, and in its few short years of availability it has become the market leader. With a handy and convenient little plastic bottle (which will not leak under any circumstances), it fits into even the smallest waistcoat pocket, and the flip-top lid makes application very simple. there is more about Gink and its methods of application in the section on Dry-fly fishing (see pp72–3).

CAR ROD CLAMPS

Fishermen the world over will always fall for a gimmick and they can easily convince themselves that even the most outrageous item of equipment is an absolute 'essential', even if it is something they will only use once in a blue moon. If we believed the tackle manufacturers about everything that they term 'essential', we would never be able to get it all in the car, let alone carry it to the waterside!

However, car rod clamps definitely are essential items. I would never be without them on any trip as they are one of the ultimate convenience items.

The principle behind car rod clamps is very simple. During the course of any day's fishing, you are likely to want to move around. You are therefore faced with the choice of tackling down your rods, which is time-consuming, or of sticking them through the car windows or sunroof while you drive to the next location. The latter is highly dangerous – more rod breakages occur in this way than any other. Many anglers with season tickets on their local waters actually leave their rods made up for the whole year, taking them to and from the lake on rod clamps, enabling them to start fishing the moment they arrive at the bankside.

For years it was the traditional firm of Wheatley that made the only clamps on the market. These were designed to fix into the rain gutters along the car roof and they could comfortably hold two or even three rods. Problems arose, however, when the motor industry redesigned car roofs in the search for greater aerodynamic efficiency. Without any thought for the angling fraternity they eliminated the rain gutters and left us with a smooth and featureless roof and nowhere to attach our rod clamps.

All the gear you need for a good day out – apart from the bottle of wine!

We were not left floundering for long, though, as this signalled the advent of the magnetic rod clamp. In many ways, this is a more efficient system, even if there was early resistance to the product – it took considerable confidence to believe that two magnets could safely hold our very expensive rods at 60mph.

These new rod clamps will fit onto any make of car (apart from the few with aluminium or glass bodies) and they do a superb job. One clamp sits on the bonnet, and this takes the butt sections. While the other sits on the roof and takes the slimmer tip sections. I have occasionally driven at up to 70mph with these clamps in total safety, although I would not suggest that anyone takes chances with them on very long journeys. If you're travelling for more than 30 miles, it would be safer to place the rods in their cases.

The best of the magnetic clamps are available from Bob Church and they can be found in most good tackle shops. Without doubt, they are a major boon to 'local' fishing, or for the lunchtime break at the pub, or when moving from Chew to Blagdon – the list is endless.

This effectively concludes an abbreviated list of tackle needed for serious stillwater fishing. I have purposely left out some seemingly obvious items, such as waistcoats and clothing, largely because of a restriction on space, but also because they are too personal to issue any meaningful guidelines. The items mentioned are, I believe, directly relevant to 'advanced' flyfishing. Without this section, what now follows on tactics would need almost continuous qualification.

PART 2

TECHNIQUE

. . . .

The wonderful thing about flyfishing is that until someone teaches trout to talk there will always be an element of uncertainty about our tactics. Nothing is beyond doubt or debate: there are no flies that work all the time and there are no elements of technique that work on every occasion.

For me, the greatest challenge in the sport, and I suppose the one thing that takes me back to the water year after year, is to work out new approaches or nuances of tactic that will catch fish. There is huge pleasure in simply being by the lakeside, but there is even greater pleasure in catching a fish as well. I have not yet reached that stage so often expounded by some writers, with a barely concealed element of piety, that it is 'enough just to be out by the water'. It is great to be out, but I still prefer a brace to a blank.

It is often said that there is a large element of luck in flyfishing. There is, indeed, a small element of luck, but as with any sport that demands application, dedication and attention to close detail, there is a far larger element of skill. It is also possible to create your own luck to a greater or lesser degree, and there will be occasions when high levels of skill are not necessary – we have all been 'lucky' enough to be on the water on those golden days when everything we throw at the fish is accepted with enthusiasm and abandon. But for most of the time it is a combination of skill, experience and commitment to the sport that will produce the best results. As Jack Nicklaus once said when someone suggested that he had been 'lucky' to sink a long putt: 'The more I practice, the luckier I get.'

This element of commitment goes hand in hand with your basic approach to the game. This book is about my core philosophies on flyfishing, which is a combination of the light line approach, blended essentially with representing or suggesting items in the trout's diet. This 'natural food' approach is not just about the flies used, but encompasses everything from lines and leaders, right through to watercraft and style of retrieve. Even such subliminal matters as attitude of mind can play their part – we all know how critical is the 'confidence' factor.

. . . .

It should also be said at the outset that there are very few short-cuts in the process of becoming a better fly fisherman. Certainly there is no substitute for experience, and the best anglers will always be those with a comprehensive memory bank of angling memories upon which they can call when the fishing is hard. Advanced flyfishing demands commitment and dedication; only then can natural ability be developed.

Far too many anglers regard the trout as little more than a catchable commodity, affording them little or no respect. This is fundamentally wrong, as without some degree of understanding of the fish, where and how they live, and when and how they feed, the angler has virtually no chance of coming to grips with them. Our quarry deserves respect, but above that we need to have an insight into their world, in all its changing moods. For instance, stock fish and resident fish behave in different ways and have different feeding patterns; it must follow, therefore, that we will need different approaches to catch them.

For this and other reasons, a brief look at the overall angling environment is called for. In addition, there are some elements of technique that need to be restated or re-examined before we move on to the finer points of tactic.

The Angling Environment

STILLWATER FISHERIES COME IN all shapes and sizes. While their character might change, with varying degrees of aesthetic appeal, there are some factors that remain constant. Thus the angler's approach can embrace some easily defined pointers that are common to all waters, the sum of which can then be linked with the variable factors of temperature, wind, weather and time of year.

CONTOUR

One of the first things to do when fishing a new water, or one that is reasonably familiar, is to look at the contour map. These are generally available in the lodges, but failing that there will normally be either bailiffs or local experts who can be tapped for information. A certain amount of information can be gained simply by studying the lie of the land, as this will give good pointers to bankside slopes and likely fishing depths, but the extra detail provided by a map is invaluable. Note the obvious features such as inlet streams, submerged river-beds or old hedge lines, as well as the not-so-obvious areas of shallow water or extreme depth. Check also for likely sources of terrestrial insects, such as withy crops, bankside bushes or copses. Remember that seemingly featureless fields can produce a lot of terrestrial life – dung flies in the summer or crane flies in September.

STYLE

Every water has its own style, whether it be an upland lake or a lowland reservoir. The latter will probably have richer water, with good run-off from farming activities, whereas the former is more likely to be thin or even acidic from peat. Trout growth and quality is directly related to the amount of food available and thus to the insect life that any water will support.

WATER QUALITY

This is the most vital factor from an angling viewpoint. It will normally determine the quality of the fishing itself, in that a good water quality, with balanced nutrients and freedom from excessive farming run-off, will support good fly life. This in turn will (generally) encourage active fish movement, coupled with surface feeding activity. Poor water quality, which is sadly an increasing fact of life these days, will cause problems: over-enrichment from intense farming run-off can ultimately cause eutrophication. In lesser cases it will still affect the fishing, causing algae blooms to varying degrees and encouraging excessive weed growth.

The angling environment is fragile, as indeed is the ecology of the British countryside. With the incorrect use of fertilisers, a problem compounded by some ludicrous EEC farming policies in the late 1980s, the whole balance of the water system can be upset. Regrettably, I do not have to look too far to see an example of this: in my own valley, Blagdon Lake has undergone a radical change in the last six years. In a lake that had a beautifully balanced ecology, with a superbly varied fly life, there came intense farming activity on the south shore. In six short years to 1991, we saw huge green algae blooms, the destruction of a massive corixa population and an almost unbelievable growth of choking blanket weed. Growth of both bankside and rooted aquatic weed simply exploded, to an extent where almost the entire lake became unfishable from the bank in high summer.

After some battles with the farm owners and some serious pressure from anglers, things started to improve after 1991, but it will take many years before Blagdon returns to her former glory. In 1980 I would happily have dipped a cup in Blagdon Lake to take a drink; in 1990 the smell of the water was enough to deter such a gesture. We can only hope that improvements will continue and that maybe the corixa will return.

Corixa

Unfortunately, not all waters are run with such care and without the good offices of the Bristol Water Company, I suspect that Blagdon would still be suffering. Larger waters, and Loch Leven is a classic example, are harder to control. What used to be a paragon among fisheries, and probably one of Britain's most famous stillwaters, is rapidly degenerating into a semi-stagnant pond due to the misuse of water quality. Effluents are flowing into it, as is sewage. Fish no longer rise there, and there were reports of serious fish-kills in 1990 as a direct result of heavy pollution. The only way to catch fish there these days is by fast sinking line, and even then the chances of success are slim.

· ·

Adrift on Leven, with the village of Kinross in the background

The outlandish colour pattern on the Parmachene Belle. Do fish actually see the colour, or is it the contrast that attracts them?

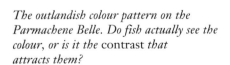

Brownies like this can only grow on with careful fishery management

. . . .

I cite these examples for several reasons, but mostly because it points up the responsibility that we have an anglers to monitor water quality. We use the water more than most, and no other band of people is in a better position to keep an eye on things. We must stand up and shout when things go seriously wrong and not just adopt the typically British head-in-the-sand attitude of wait-and-see, or leaving it to someone else. Without our voice, coupled with that of bodies such as the ACA, some farmers and landowners will continue to take liberties and will continue to get away with it. This is not meant in any way to denigrate such people, and indeed the majority care for the environment as much if not more than we do, but there is an element that sees land and water as merely resources to be exploited in the short term, regardless of the consequences.

Expressing my personal opinion is not included here out of context, as there are positive steps that anglers can take to improve and maintain our water quality. It is our responsibility to protect the angling environment for this and future generations, and there is far too much apathy in our ranks. The more prominent we become as fishermen, the greater will be our voice – if we fail to use that voice now, there will be little point in complaining when it is too late. What nearly happened at Blagdon can and will happen elsewhere.

Thankfully, water quality in Britain is still reasonably good and, compared to many European counterparts, it is excellent. It is up to us to fight for the preservation of that status.

WATER CLARITY

Inevitably, this is linked with water quality, but it is very much another matter from an angling viewpoint. Some of our waters are naturally very clear, while others (for varying reasons) are not. The actual clarity of the water will affect how we fish, the flies that we fish, and often the depth that we fish. Bright and gaudy flies can have a scaring effect on the trout in very clear water, whereas those same flies are necessary to provide extra visibility in water that is murky, clouded by wind or wave action, or suffering from an algae bloom. Similarly, we are likely to need all the benefits of low-diameter nylon in gin-clear water, yet on others it may well pay us to use standard monofilament.

The point about bright flies needs further expansion and it is very much an angling 'variable'. On waters such as Rutland, which is normally very clear, there are times when bright flies like the Peach Doll or flashy flies such as Silver Invicta will not work, despite that they are normally proven patterns for that water. A combination of bright sun and very clear water will almost always demand a more sombre fly, and it is at times like these that the smaller imitative patterns are at their best. In cloudy water, perhaps coupled with low light conditions, the trout's vision range is reduced, and in consequence we will have need of a fly with high visibility. It is not an infallible rule-of-thumb, but the heavy fluorescent colours do not normally link with very clear water.

Another variable in very clear water concerns speed of retrieve. It follows that a fly that can be seen for some distance is also a fly that the fish can inspect very closely, if not at his leisure. In such circumstances it is not always wise to make things easier for the fish by giving them too much time; a faster retrieve pattern will force the fish into a decision, giving him less time to study the deficiencies in the fly and less time to choose.

The reverse of this can be true in cloudy water as the fly will be visible to the fish for a relatively short time. This is particularly true when fishing the sunk line at depth where light is drastically reduced and where a slow retrieve is almost obligatory.

FEEDING PATTERNS

With trout, anglers are competing with a creature that is totally at home in his environment. He has sight and scent to help him locate his food items, as well as the added bonus of 'touch' through his lateral line. He is supremely sensitive to change and will react very quickly to even the lightest insect hatch.

Apart from very recent stock fish, and by this I mean fish that have been in the water for three days or less, I think that anglers do not accord the trout the full measure of respect that they deserve. Residential trout, either brown or rainbow, become residential because they have survived all natural predations, but also because they have been able to avoid the myriad of artificial flies that get thrown at them every day of the season. I suggest, therefore, that we should gear our approach very much towards these residents, on the principle that if a less educated fish gets in the way, then so much the better. This seemingly simplistic view fits in well with the light line approach, and particularly with a range of flies geared to imitating natural food items, but it also pre-supposes that we have at least a working knowledge of the trout's feeding patterns.

There is an almost constant reference to feeding patterns throughout this book, and again they are very variable. Feeding trout will take food items at any time of day and at any depth of water – those anglers who declare that the fish are 'not feeding' simply because they are not showing on the surface are only seeing a very small part of the picture. There are, however, still some 'constant' factors to rely upon, or at least to be aware of, such as the fabled morning and evening rises.

The reason that we have such good morning or evening rises is twofold. First, it is a natural feeding pattern that coincides with heavy insect life and activity. Trout have recognised periods of inactivity both at day- and night-time, and these traditional 'rises' occur at the end of such periods. The second reason is that they can see the food items more clearly at a time of relatively low light. It has been proven that trout have eyes that are sensitive to strong light, just as our own. For instance, we all know that when we are boat fishing the trout are notoriously reluctant to move upwind into a bright sun, yet in equally bright light they are happy to feed when they are facing away from the sun. It is one of the great truisms of fishing that we are more likely to see a good rise on a gentle overcast day than one when the sun shines brightly. What is not so generally appreciated is that on those same bright days the fish are still likely to be feeding, but at varied depths. The reluctance of many anglers to reach for the armoury of sinking lines, to explore the depths with different flies and retrieve methods, or simply to believe that the fish are feeding, is the reason why there are so many blanks on days of bright sunshine.

FOOD ITEMS

I do not propose to go into any great dissertations on insect orders or other food items that make up the diet of stillwater trout. This has been covered thoroughly by other authors, and in any event it would be insulting to suggest that anyone aspiring to advanced flyfishing does not already possess such knowledge. I hope I can assume, therefore, that any reader of this book has at least a working knowledge of the principal insects, their life cycles and preferred habitats, and their relevance to the fish. Anyone who cannot recognise the difference between a damsel and a dragonfly nymph, who does not know what a free-swimming sedge pupa looks like, or who cannot distinguish between a dung fly and a hawthorn has some further reading to do.

Damsel nymph

As we shall see later, there are occasions when the trout will eat virtually anything that they can find on or in the water, including such delicacies as cigarette butts. However, what really concerns us here are the more staple diet items, in all the stages of their life cycle. These are fully covered in the section on spooning (see Part 3), but it is not so widely known that you can make a fair guess as to what the fish are feeding on purely by studying the way in which they rise. This relates to all feeding activity on the surface, as well as to a certain amount of sub-surface feeding down to depths of 2–3ft: not all rise forms involve the fish breaking through the water surface.

So, after a necessarily brief look at the overall environment for angling, we can now move on to the specific elements of technique that contribute to advanced flyfishing. The rise that the fish makes as it feeds is so significant and contains so much information that is useful to the angler, that it makes an ideal link point in this chapter.

Rise Forms

THE WAY THAT A trout rises can be analysed in some detail. The various rise forms not only provide indicators of feeding depth but also of the actual food item being taken – a vital consideration. By definition they do, of course, betray the very presence of fish in any given area, which can be an additional bonus in the case of waters like Rutland; on smaller stillwaters the fish are more inclined to rise over the entire lake, whereas on the larger expanses localised hatches result in localised rising. Each rise form has its own significance, and although rises can at first appear to be completely haphazard, they can in fact be categorised.

SUB-SURFACE RISES

A rise is not a rise when it occurs at depths of 2–3ft, without any real breaking of the water surface, leaving scarcely any surface disturbance to betray the fish's presence.

Sub-surface rises, or boils as they are sometimes called, are almost always caused by fish taking midge or sedge pupae. They will often take place when there is a chill factor at the surface, which sends the pupae back to the depths or leaves them in the cooler surface water layer. In conditions like this the pupae do not hatch and are left in a 'limbo' state; either they sink slowly back to the bottom or they are left static in the top few feet of water, where the fish are happy to mop them up.

The interesting thing to watch for at times like this is the percentage of boils to proper rises. There may be a few genuine head-and-tails, but a higher percentage of boils is a strong indicator that the pupae should be fished rather than the adult insect. Often an evening rise can be killed by a chilly breeze to the extent where the fish stop feeding off the top. Even so, they are still around, and far too many anglers pack up too early at such times. The answer is to use either weighted pupae or patterns tied on heavy wire hooks to reach down those few vital feet: light wire hooks or surface film pupae are not going to reach the fish.

Boils and deeper sub-surface 'rises' are notoriously hard to spot. Sometimes there will be a heaving on the surface that is quite noticeable, but on other occasions there will only be a little flattening of the water surface, and this is hard to see from any distance. In extreme cases there will only be a tiny variance in the ripple pattern to look out for, and these are sometimes referred to as 'innuendoes' rather than rises. My policy in such cases is simple: it is far better to cast to an innuendo than to nothing at all.

If sub-surface boils do occur, then it is worth remembering that the flies are just as likely to be taken as they sink as when they are being retrieved. Pupae often make many journeys to the surface before they finally decide to hatch, and if they encounter inhospitable conditions, they just allow themselves to sink slowly to the bottom again, without any of the thrashing movements that they use to propel themselves to the surface. In these instances, a 'free fall' buzzer pattern can be a very close copy indeed.

It is not fair to say that all sub-surface rises are to sedge or midge, although I would suggest that about 90 per cent of them probably are. Some may well be to damsel, or even to fry, and the key as always is observation. This, coupled with the vital evidence of the marrow scoop, is the crux of the matter.

THE SIP

Sometimes referred to as a dimpling rise, this occurs to a variety of food items and as such is potentially confusing. By definition, though, it is a very positive rise form, with a clear purpose to it: to remove an item from the water surface. Sipping rises tend to take place in calmer conditions, and it should be possible for the angler to see the food items for himself, if not actually to pick one off the surface for examination.

Sipping rises take place at any time during the day and can be instigated by a range of weather conditions. The disappearance of a breeze may result in adult insects landing on the water in some numbers. Alternatively, the advent of a chilly breeze in the later evening can have the same result. Falls of terrestrial insects such as ants or dung flies can occur, as well as the ubiquitous crane flies. All of these insects can pro-

Left: *A top-class fish for Terry Griffiths, consultant editor for* Stillwater Trout Angler

Right: *Just before the net at Rutland*

voke a precise sipping rise, in conditions when the fish have plenty of time to examine them before taking, and unfortunately in plenty of time to reject an artificial one.

My rule-of-thumb for sipping risers is definitely to scale down the line diameter, and probably the fly size as well. Sipping fish are fussy fish and they have plenty of time to look at the fly's deficiencies.

THE NEBBING RISE

By contrast, the nebbing rise is more likely to occur in rougher conditions of wind or wave, or at the very least in a good ripple. The food items are the same – virtually anything – but the fish have less time to view them and to make up their minds as to whether or not they are edible. The nebbing rise is the 'general' rise form, or the 'typical' rise, if you like.

I was once of the opinion that it was possible to determine a trout's cruising depth by looking at the rings from a typical nebbing rise, but I am no longer convinced. The theory was that trout rising from any depth made larger forward bulging rings. It was a nice theory and on occasions of flat calm it still has some merit. However, in any sort of ripple it is not reliable as there are simply too many variables.

By definition, the nebbing rise involves some part of the fish – usually his nose or neb – breaking through the surface. The food item may be trapped in the film (terrestrials or spent adults) or they may be pupae on the point of hatching. Again, it is the evidence of the marrow spoon that is vital, coupled with the necessary observation of the water. In the vast majority of instances this rise form involves fish that are cruising very high in the water, with a total preoccupation with surface food items. It follows therefore that flies fished at any depth are of no use and that conditions demand the dries.

The glorious thing about nebbing fish is their predictability. Rise forms like this are not only easy to see, but it is also possible to see the fish's direction of travel. Ambushes can be laid and forward lead can be employed, all to good effect.

THE HEAD AND TAIL

Of all the rise forms on stillwater, this must surely be the one we all long to see. It is a full-blooded, no-holds-barred rise form, implying a total commitment on the part of the fish to take the food item. It is a rise form that takes place with complete abandon, and in almost any water and weather conditions.

The head and tail is, of course, the easiest rise form to see. The whole of the fish, or at least all of it that is above the lateral line, will break through the surface in one long fluid motion. The fish will be cruising high in the water and taking surface food items with some precision. Again, the combination of eyesight and marrow scoop will provide the pointers to fly selection, and almost certain a dry fly will be required.

The most important thing about head-and-tailing fish will be the accuracy of the cast – the actual fly pattern will be of secondary importance. The truth of this is clearly demonstrated in a caenis hatch, or even when the fish are head and tailing through daphnia swarms: on these occasions they will happily take a well-presented hopper, even though it bears no resemblance to the food item that instigated the rise. As they are so high in the water, their 'window' is drastically reduced.

Head-and-tailing fish are nothing if not predictable. An individual fish will often hold a straight line for ten or more rises, making both ambushes and tight forward lead casts possible.

THE SLASHING RISE

This is sometimes mistakenly referred to as the 'fry-basing' rise, which is wrong because it is by no means restricted to fry-feeding fish. It is also the most difficult rise to predict, as it is almost completely haphazard in its nature and location.

The slashing rise can consist of anything from a vicious turning boil on the surface, to a crashing leap that takes the fish several feet into the air. When trout are feeding on fry (typically from June to September), they will often chase them into the margins from some depth, culminating in this rise form within a few feet of the bank. Equally, it can occur just as easily in open water, or over shallow points or weed-banks.

Towards the end of the season the fish can become totally preoccupied with fry as a food item, using this as a useful bounty ahead of the long winter months. It is a very distinctive rise form, often preceded by a shower of fry just before the fish breaks surface. Trout will often return after the initial savage rise to pick up stunned victims in a much more leisurely fashion, so a floating fry pattern fished static can be just as useful as pulled fry imitators.

Slashing rises also occur when other large food items are about, most notable among them being the craneflies. However, I have seen this rise form to mayfly, dung fly and even to individual red midge, so an open mind is called for rather than an arbitrary assumption that fry are the food item in question.

The identification of rise forms is just a small part of that all-embracing term 'watercraft', so often referred to as some mystical ability that only a few near-saints possess. In fact, the crucial elements in watercraft are clearly definable, as we shall now see.

Watercraft

IN ITS SIMPLEST FORM, watercraft is about nothing more than angling common sense. At the other end of the scale, it comes down to a combination of gut-feelings, instinct and the application of fishing experience, all of which affect the approach to each day's fishing. The key to successful flyfishing lies in the interpretation of each new set of circumstances at the waterside and of pulling together all the variables to arrive at a meaningful set of tactics for any given situation. All of which sounds just a little too glib and a little too clear-cut, so it is worth reminding the reader that the experts have their bad days too, when nothing goes right, and no amount of clever thought and planning makes the slightest bit of difference. Top quality watercraft will not turn impossible conditions into ideal ones; it will, however, turn reasonable days into very good ones.

At the risk of sounding repetitive, I must assume for the purposes of this book that the reader will already have the basics under his belt. The more obvious aspects of watercraft such as careful wading, the ability to sit quietly and cast properly from a boat, and the ability to 'read' bankside contour – all of these are taken for granted. Some aspects of watercraft do, however, require further elaboration.

FOOD CHANNELS

The bankside configuration is normally fairly easy to read, as in most cases it is a mirror image of the bank contour above water level. Inlet flows and streams are obvious variants, as are the areas of rapid fall-off to deeper water that can be identified either from maps of the lake or by studying the lake when water levels are low. The latter represents time well spent, but do make notes – it is notoriously difficult to recall particular features when levels return to normal.

It is less well known that bays and promontories can form very positive food channels, in varying wind conditions. In conditions of high winds, it is easy to see the

Charles Jardine uses tall reeds to screen him from the fish

mud slicks that form downwind of points, or along the windward banks. In lesser winds the mud may not be there, but the food most certainly is, pushed by the ripple into relatively concentrated lanes. Trout tend to hold in these 'flow areas', gratefully accepting the increased food level for no extra effort. Obvious downwind concentrations of daphnia are one thing, but food channels are quite another: they can form in unusual places, with sub-surface currents taking food well out from a seemingly featureless bank, just because the underwater contour has a marked variation. The effect of this is clearly visible at Rutland at Three Trees (Normanton), at Grafham by the Sludge Lagoons and at Bewl in the Nose.

With any kind of prevailing wind, the actual flow of the water increases dramatically around points or promontories, and again the fish like to hold in this increased flow. As in the rivers, this brings the food to them for a minimal expenditure of effort. This increase is not just restricted to points, as downwind banks will often have a much faster flow within a few yards of the bank than there will be 10yd out. When boat fishing, it is almost always worth drifting right into the shore (or as close as local rules and bank anglers will permit) to explore this phenomenon. Common courtesy obviously prohibits this when bank anglers are in the vicinity.

WIND LANES

Wind lanes are like high-density food larders for the fish. There are contrasting theories as to why they form, but the reasons do not matter at all. The fact is that they do form and that the trout love them. Not only do these lanes hold more food, but that same food is also much more visible to the fish by virtue of the calm water surrounding it. A further bonus is that the ripple that exists everywhere else acts as a sight screen for the angler, whether he be on a boat or on a bank, giving some real camouflage.

Scum lanes are similar, but significantly different. In character they are generally more narrow than wind lanes, forming in higher winds into serried ranks. Indeed, some wind lanes can look like great motorways on the water, and it is often the case that the wider they get the less useful they are to the angler. Scum lanes are often shunned by anglers, whereas in fact they are extremely good news: far from putting the fish off, as some anglers believe, they act as a screen, allowing the fish to move with even more confidence than they do in a normal wind lane. When the wind picks up, and as soon as the scum lanes begin to form, make sure that your flies are in among them.

SHALLOWS

To the boat fisherman, knowledge of the lake contour is nothing less than vital. He needs to be able to identify areas of underwater shallows, false islands and old river courses. These areas are holding stations not just for the trout, but also for the things upon which trout feed.

Indicators of such places do not just come from contour maps, and such maps are not always available. Feeding birds can be a giveaway: nothing makes the Roman Shallows easier to find on Chew in May than the sight of twenty or more swans, tails up and necks down, feeding on the emerging weed-beds. In similar vein, grebes and gulls betray the presence of fish fry, and such fry prefer to shoal around some sort of feature underwater, even if it is nothing more than a weed-bed.

Apart from being a huge bonus in terms of their beauty – and I get as much pleasure sometimes from watching the birds as I do from the fishing – all the lake birds are of interest to the angler. Swifts and swallows are often the first to spot a hatch of fly, even before the trout, and their stooping to the water indicates hatching adult insects. As well as diving for fry, the gulls will also indicate hatches of flying ants in summer by wheeling high, and in the late evenings on Chew it is the duck that feed most avidly on the buzzers, giving a sure indication that the adult insects are lying spent on the water surface.

FOOTSTEPS

It is always worth remembering that the natural habitat of trout will invariably be the lake margins – it is only the pressure of anglers that sends them to the middle of the reservoir. If it were not for the hundreds of size 10 waders, then the margins of our lakes would be teeming throughout the year; for this reason alone, my favourite time at Blagdon used to be the first few hours of the new day, when no anglers were about, and my waders never used to get wet. Disturbance is the watercraft element here, and he who wades lightly and casts a light line will be the one with the most fish. Etiquette is also relevant, and a man stealthily fishing a weed-bed should be given enough room to enjoy his sport undisturbed, just as you would wish for yourself.

THE 10ft MARKER

I have a theory, well proven to my own satisfaction, that trout have a distinct preference for water that is about 10ft deep. It is their ideal living depth, with room enough to escape predators (including fishermen), plenty of light for food visibility and plenty of room for manoeuvre. Time and again I have found fish on the 10ft marker, when other depths have been barren. This has great relevance to both boat and bank anglers, but perhaps even more so on the bank. It will pay to determine whether the 'mark' can be reached by long or short wading, or indeed if wading is needed at all.

Depth-sounders are not yet available on stillwater boats – thank goodness. In their absence, and in the absence of any other suitable tool, you will often see serious anglers poking their (very expensive) rods into the water to determine the depth at which they are fishing. This apparently amateurish way of establishing the depth is a major factor in fishing, and other decisions on line and leader configurations come from it. For me, though, it is about one crucial factor alone: I really like fishing on the 10ft mark.

CAMOUFLAGE

For most anglers, the only thoughts about camouflage are those concerned with wearing drab clothing, and maybe a quick thought about using some bankside vegetation as cover. It is sad that things rarely progress much further than that. Yet the camouflage factor can be taken so much further. All bankside features will help to conceal the angler from the fish, or at the very least they will help to break up the skyline view. Underwater ledges are even better; fish like to hold beneath them, and this effectively cuts their 'window' in half.

By far the best natural camouflage is the weed-bed, and this is just as relevant to the boat fisherman as it is to the one fishing from the bank. It is perfectly possible to creep up on rising fish by using the weed-bed as a screen, allowing very close casts to be made.

As we saw when discussing wind lanes, ripple is also an effective camouflage, particularly when you are fishing near to those little calm patches that so often appear for no obvious reason. My preference when fishing the wind lanes is to fish their edges rather than their middle. Although they rise all over the lanes, the fish tend to hold the edges more readily, and I find it more productive to fish into the lanes at an angle rather than straight down them. The significant factor here is undoubtedly camouflage.

Camouflage: crouching to avoid 'skylining' and using the shade of the tree

CHANGE DAYS

Of all the 'exterior' factors – that is, those beyond our control – that affect the fishing, weather must surely be at the top of the list. You will often hear pundits claiming very widely that you must 'read the water' before setting out, yet their own reading does not extend far beyond watching the weather forecast on the preceding evening. In reality, reading the water involves a serious matching of wind, waves, cloud, sun and rain, with all the seasonal factors of projected (expected) fly life and lake contour. More often than not, the weather determines the success or otherwise of the day.

Prevailing weather conditions are referred to constantly throughout this book, together with suitable tactics to match them. There are days, however, that are not in any way quantifiable, and for want of a better term I refer to them as 'change days'. Change days are, very simply, the days of transition from one set of weather conditions to another. It can be as dramatic as the advent of a new weather system, or as little as a change in prevailing winds. In most cases, the fish don't like them; nothing plays greater havoc with fish-feeding patterns than abrupt weather changes. Overnight frost, sudden chill winds, and even sudden changes in wind direction will send fish to the bottom, and the effects of the change day can last for some time.

In my experience, the worst changes are those which take place during the day rather than overnight. I have been on Chew with fish rising all over the place, with the wind blowing away from the sun. A change of wind direction of less than 20° has completely killed the fishing, even though all other factors of temperature and cloud cover remained the same.

Paul Canning concentrates on a varied retrieve

Reading the weather is one of the prime considerations of watercraf

Obviously, there is nothing we can do about such changes, except to be aware of them and to be prepared for a fundamental change of tactics. Scrutiny of weather forecasts is obligatory, but of greater importance is the flexibility of approach that permits a total change of fishing depth, with new line, leader and flies at a moment's notice.

Retrieves

IN ALMOST ANY CONVERSATION about flyfishing tactics you will hear a lot of talk about retrieves. People have different ideas about speed, depth and style of retrieve, and there are as many opinions as there are anglers. Many fishermen get very serious and preoccupied about fly patterns, but in fact it is how you move the fly that is more important. The retrieve is vital: it is not the fly, but how it moves that really counts.

Beginners or newcomers to the sport can be forgiven for thinking that it is all a matter of casting a fly out as far as possible and then stripping it back at a constant speed. In the early days, there is enough to think about in getting your casting right, without the added complication of worrying about retrieves.

Once you have mastered the basics, it is vital to give thought to how your fly is performing either on or under the water. When talking about fly patterns you will hear the expression that such and such a feather will add 'life' to the fly, and this simple word contains the real secret. All the different retrieves are designed to enhance the movement or appeal of the fly, giving it a lifelike appearance, and fooling the fish into thinking that it is food rather than a concoction of metal and feather.

This may sound rather simplistic, but you would be surprised at how many anglers overlook this basic fact. I have seen beginners trying to strip back a buzzer pupa or even trying to fish a fry imitator with a figure-of-eight: on an odd occasion both these just might work, but they come a long way down on the list of probabilities.

There are almost as many styles of retrieve as your imagination will allow. Some are established favourites, whereas others are new. A few are genuine innovations, the product of today's new generation of intelligent fly fishermen who are always on the lookout for a new method to give them the edge on the fish. Trout very quickly get used to seeing all our lures and flies, and in three weeks after stocking they can become well educated. Anglers who try for them with a monotonous, regular, unvaried retrieve will not be likely to score.

Within all these varied methods, however, there are still some clearly identifiable retrieves that we can qualify and describe. The list contains some of the most traditional names in flyfishing that will strike a chord with anglers of all ages.

STATIC RETRIEVE

This is not a contradiction of the Trades Description Act, as there are many instances where the retrieve is as near-static as possible. Static retrieve is used mostly in late evening, when a team of buzzers can be cast out and just left in the surface film. Similarly, in high summer when the fish are fry bashing, it will often pay to cast a single fry imitator into the boil and leave it static. The third instance is in dry-fly fishing, when either a team or a single fly can be employed. However, in all these instances it is important to keep in touch with your line and not to allow a big bow to form. Consequently, you may need to retrieve a little line, even if you are not actually moving the flies themselves – hence the name.

FIGURE-OF-EIGHT

Probably the slowest of all retrieves, this is for gently nymphing or for teams of flies in very calm conditions. The line is gathered in one hand in a series of tight double loops, looking like a figure-of-eight in the hand. A variation often found on stillwater is to let these loops drop into the water as they form while still using the very slow retrieve movement.

PULL AND PAUSE

This can be anything from very slow to medium speed and is probably the most common form of retrieve in use today. It is used for all types of fishing, from nymphs to wet flies, or from buzzers to lures. The line is retrieved in a series of short pulls with little pauses in between each pull. The length of the pulls can and should be varied, from a few inches to a foot or more. For instance, nymphs can be pulled about 5–6 in at a time, while larger lures or lead-heads will need longer, sharper pulls. Flies can be given an attractive ascent/descent movement by lengthening the pauses.

MILKING THE COW

This vulgar-sounding expression is the term often used to describe the constant retrieve. The rod is tucked under one arm and the line pulled back in one long movement by a hand-over-hand retrieve. From any distance it looks as though the angler is going through a 'milking the cow' motion – hence the name. This method is popular among lead-head fishers as it makes the marabou tail feathers work well. We all know how often fish will take just as we are reeling in, and this style of retrieve exploits this to the full. It has particular relevance when we want fry imitators or damsels pulled at a constant speed.

SINK AND HOLD

This method is used generally in boat fishing, although it can also be good on deep, steep-sided banks. It employs the sinking line, which is cast out and allowed to sink to the required depth. It is then quickly retrieved until the line is near-vertical beneath the angler. It is then held for a few seconds before a series of short pulls brings it jerkily to the surface. Takes often come at the point of lift-off as this method is almost like dibbling beneath the surface, and combines all the benefits of the 'induced take'.

An alternative to this, usually with a slow sinking line, is known as FTA, or 'fool them about'. The line sinks a little way down and is then brought back with a series of erratic and varied pulls, interspersed with pauses of varying length. This works best with lures, but is also good with moving nymphs or attractors such as damsels or montanas. In essence, it is an unpredictable retrieve and keeps the fish guessing.

STRIPPING

This is the fastest retrieve of all and is mostly confined to lure fishing in the summer months when fish are prepared to chase a fly. It is used on both floating and sinking lines, and the former is very exciting as you can see the bow wave as the fish chases the fly, often with his nose only inches away from it.

Stripping is also used in boat fishing, although for different reasons. In a big wind, the boat will be drifting so fast that the angler has to strip just to keep up with the line, and in fact his actual retrieve of the flies is really quite slow.

These are the basic types and styles of retrieve in use on most waters, and all the other methods are really only variations on the same theme or at best are individual methods invented for individual fisheries. These descriptions will give you a good idea of how to match them to the type of fishing you intend to do and also with the fly patterns in use.

Above all, the fundamental thing to remember is that you are only trying to give 'life' to your flies – that is the one main reason for the retrieve. Even the best tied flies will be useless without a well thought out retrieve matched to the prevailing conditions.

Colin Moynihan with a 4lb Rainbow

PART 3

TACTICS

This section of the book is devoted exclusively to tactics. The preceding pages have been a necessity and have, I hope, laid some of the foundations for what follows.

One reviewer of my last book, *Success with Trout*, wrote that the section on competitions was far too short. In fact, the whole book was devoted to the tactics and techniques involved in competition fishing; my angling philosophy does not change just because the day is 'competitive' as opposed to 'normal'. In fact, anyone who tried to cultivate two separate styles of fishing would soon be left floundering, and it is only because I genuinely believe that competitions are good for the future of our sport that I support them so fully. This means that virtually all my fishing is done with small flies and in a style that conforms to the set of rules – a code of ethics for anglers – laid down by the international bodies.

In the same way, the whole of this book relates to the tactics and methods that I employ, including the section on tackle. Without a total appreciation of the make-up of the sport – and this embraces rods and leader configurations in the same way as it does floating or sinking line methods – the angler is left with only a part of the picture.

To some established anglers I suspect that parts of what follows will be old hat, although I hope that they will argue with some of the methods that are expounded: without a healthy dialogue and debate, the whole business of angling would soon become too quantifiable. As individuals, we all seek different aspects of pleasure from our sport, which is as it should be. If a finite level of expertise could be reached, then flyfishing would quickly lose its charm and appeal. Thankfully it cannot, so I can only put forward 'my' style as one interpretation among many.

Some of the sub-chapters here involve small nuances of tactic, while others are fundamentally significant methods in their own right. The dry-fly section falls into the latter category, and this piece, like all others, should be read in conjunction with the full description of the flies concerned that follows at the end of the book. I have purposely separated the flies rather than include them in individual sections, for ease of reading.

Nowadays a complete fly box is devoted to stillwater dries

Long wading is not always a good idea: this fish took in the margins, with water scarcely over the angler's ankles

Stillwater Dries

SO MUCH HAS BEEN written over the last few years about the use of dry fly on still-water that we could easily be forgiven for thinking that it is a recent invention. Writers have enthused over the method, using words like 'innovative' and 'discovery' to such an extent that they give the distinct impression that it is a modern phenomenon. In fact, dry fly has existed for many years and was enjoying huge popularity on Blagdon as early as the 1950s. Rediscovery is one thing, but 'invention' is something else entirely.

That said, it is undeniable that there has been some considerable pioneering work done at the tying bench by the exponents of stillwater dries. During the long hot summer of 1990, use of the dries reached an unprecedented level, achieving a status akin to a cult fever: it was *the* method to use and lesser mortals who stuck to simple pulling flies or sunk line were looked upon pityingly, or in extreme cases as second-class citizens. The feeling was almost that if you weren't using dries, you weren't really fishing. There was just a hint of fly-fishing snobbery about!

The good thing about all this was that everyone quickly realised that the use of stillwater dry fly required no special skills and was not nearly as complex as had first been supposed. The basic flies were now obtainable in most fishing lodges and tackle shops, and with virtually no adjustments to the standard floating-line gear, anglers found that they could enjoy the method. In view of the visual excitement that it provides, coupled with the fact that it is such a wonderfully relaxed way of fishing, it is hardly surprising that it has captured everyone's imagination at such a rate.

However, most people realised that there was much more to this method than simply casting out a team of flies and then waiting for something to happen. True, you could catch fish that way, but with a little thought and experimentation the catch rate could be dramatically improved. Shop-bought flies were found to be less than effective in fussy conditions, and a rethink was needed on the subject of presentation. Similarly, a revision of opinion on leader formats was required, and those who used an AFTM 5 instead of a 7 were rewarded with vastly improved results. All of these points helped when fishing the dries, but none were so fundamentally important as the flies themselves, and it is here that the real work has been done. A mere handful of anglers have made a genuine contribution to the sport and the word 'innovation' really does apply to their fly-tying work.

Inevitably, much of the pioneering work was done by those involved in the competition scene. To succeed in competitions needs a high level of commitment and application, and while these factors may be present in competitors' everyday fishing, they will always need a certain 'edge' on match days. Consequently, a long hard look was taken at the established dry-fly patterns, and slowly these evolved into something very different and substantially better.

But this is jumping ahead somewhat: perhaps I should put things in perspective by saying that I have been using dries on stillwater for some fifteen years. In those early days it was looked upon as something rather eccentric and nobody could really understand why I was wasting my time with a solitary rising brownie that was totally preoccupied with adult sedge, when there were plenty of rainbows to be had with nymph. I used to get a mixture of raised eyebrow looks, liberally mixed with muttered comments of 'purist' and the like. It did not matter because above all I was having fun, using a single fly on a long leader, trying to extract recalcitrant browns from the depths of Blagdon's Orchard Bay, with a difficulty factor that went off the scale.

The flies that I used then bear little resemblance to those in use today. Indeed, it is a sobering thought to recall that dry flies occupied barely two rows in the corner of my box, whereas these days I have two full boxes devoted exclusively to them. The favourite was a little squirrel tail sedge, tied on a size 14 light wire hook from Partridge. It was a simple tying, with a pheasant tail fibre body, and a light brown head hackle, clipped across the bottom so that it sat nicely in the water. The wing of natural squirrel tail was clipped into the roof-shape of the adult sedge, and in fact the colour mix of brown and grey was a fairly close copy of the grouse wings that were so prolific on Blagdon. More than any of my early dries, that one has stood the test of time and is still as effective today.

The fly also underlines another popular myth that needs to be dispelled, as many people seem to think that dries are only for boat work and have little relevance on the bank. On the contrary: much of my dry-fly research has been carried out on the bank, where the challenge is perhaps even greater than in the boat. Presentation and accuracy are vital, but above all else the fly has to be right, in profile, silhouette and colour. If the fly works on the bank, it is virtually guaranteed to be good in the boats.

Before looking at some of the latest flies in depth, it is worth making a point about presentation. With 'pulling' tactics, it is not nearly as crucial to have the flies landing properly: if things are rather wayward, two or three pulls will straighten the leader. With the dries, and particularly when casting accurately at moving fish, it is vital that the team lands in a straight line with good turnover of the leader. This can be achieved by 'stopping' the line with the left hand, just before the end of the cast. This simple action tightens the line and loop, ensuring that the leader turns over cleanly on every cast. With a little practice it becomes second nature and the flies land well spaced every time.

You will also need to have a slight rethink about leaders, as a few minor changes can make a big difference. Almost all my dry-fly work is done with super-strength nylon. Not only is it obviously finer, and therefore does not intrude into the silhouette of the fly itself, but it is also more supple. Because presentation is so important – far more so than with any other style – super-strength nylon is a must. The leader formats are shown in the diagram and relate to fishing a team of dries. A point worth stressing is that the droppers are noticeably longer than for conventional wet-fly work, at around 8–9in.

On occasions, there is a strong case for fishing an individual dry fly as opposed to a team. On really fussy days, and notably in the impossible flat calm, a single fly is the only way to achieve perfect presentation. Taper the leader as fine as you dare, certainly down to 4lb super strength or below, and present the fly as far away from the boat or bank as possible. Fish get suspicious in flat calms and a solitary fly arouses fewer alarm signals than even a perfectly presented team of two.

One final point on leaders concerns the 'degreasing' process. This general term is also taken to include removing the shine from the nylon, which is particularly relevant to

LEADER FORMATS FOR STILLWATER DRY FLY

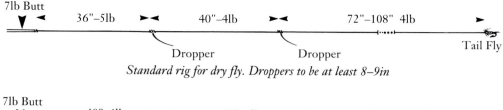

Standard rig for dry fly. Droppers to be at least 8–9in

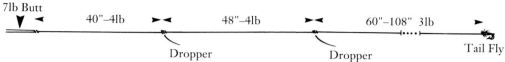

Rig for balanced fishing, on fussy days, typically with emergers on droppers, and hopper on point.
Droppers to be 8–9in

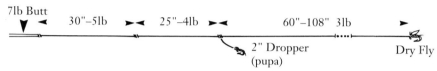

'Hedged Bet' rig, using very short dropper of only 2in for small (size 14/16) midge pupa. Cruising fish
often take the pupa in calm conditions, and the dry fly then acts as a strike indicator

super strength. You will need to take much more care over this than you would, say, for normal floating-line work. Contrary to the popular belief held by some, the leader needs to sink and not to float. If it floats, it looks like a hawser in the trout's window and totally negates all other aspects of presentation. You will need to pinch and roll the leader between forefinger and thumb, with a good application of mud (or Fuller's Earth mix), as well as pulling it through at least half-a-dozen times. Much of the time you will be laying an ambush for the fish with the dries: predicting his direction of travel and laying the flies well ahead so that he moves on to them. But if the leader isn't right, all the accuracy and presentation in the world will be to no avail.

And so to the flies themselves. Broadly speaking, these can be divided into two categories: dries, for fishing on the water surface, and semi-dries, for fishing in the surface. In fact, there are now relatively few flies that I tie to sit right on the top, as even the hopper is improved by tying the legs trailing well down so that it sits in the film. As their name implies, the emergers sit well down in the film, relying principally on outline and silhouette for effectiveness. Shipman-style buzzers are almost a category in their own right, as they can be just as good when fished high or low – it depends on the prevailing conditions of wind and wave. Full tying details for each pattern and indicators on when to fish them, are to found in the flies section.

Probably the first fly that comes to mind when anyone mentions dries is the hopper, and rightly so. It seems to epitomise the method and is very much a fly for all occasions. It has a general rather than a specific appeal, and is more suggestive than imitative. Just as the Pheasant Tail is the suggestive classic nymph, so too is the hopper the universal dry fly. Hoppers can be tied in a whole range of sizes, but the best fall in the range from 10 to 14. If the day looks even remotely suitable for the dries, or if you are not sure about what is hatching, then a size 12 hopper is the first choice of fly. My favourite colours for the hopper are amber and claret, while in early season black can have its day, especially if there are any hawthorns about. Later in the year, when the natural crane flies are on the water, then a size 10 with a darker grey body, badger hackle and grey legs is very useful.

Apart from the hoppers, most of the real development has been centred upon that vague group of patterns that tend to be loosely termed as 'emergers'. Fish take them confidently and often when there is little or no hatch taking place. On Grafham in particular, a team of emergers is much the best way to intercept cruising trout.

The standard emerger, or at least the Bristol interpretation of it, involves an ultra slim seal's fur body, with a tiny 'false wing', usually of white hackle fibres. It has two turns of hackle at the head, which is then clipped across the bottom to help it sit well down. The whole thing is very sparse, far more so than most commercially available patterns. These simple flies are tied in a range of colours, with a strong red/claret mix being the favourite. The favourite hook size is 14, although 12s are better in a big wave: the new Partridge grey shadow fine wire is perfect, as the grey colouring seems to improve the patterns.

The latest, and probably the best, emerger variant is the raider. This is tied with a slim seal's fur body, taken down to the hook bend, and a bulky seal's fur thorax. The silhouette is improved by picking out the fibres on the top of this thorax, again so that the fly sits well down. Claret has proved to be by far the best colour, with black also being useful earlier in the year.

Yet a further variation is to tie the raider with legs, hopper-style. The tying is exactly the same, but you add two legs on the side of the thorax, using knotted PT fibres. This seems to further enhance the 'emerger' characteristics, and is especially good in a heavy hatch or for evening fishing. A rib, either pearly or oval, is optional on all emergers and raiders.

These few flies, all of which are relatively easy to tie, form the backbone of my stillwater dry-fly selection, and it is no exaggeration to say that they are used for 95 per cent of my sport. The so-called 'specials', such as the tiny smuts, are really only for 'one-off' occasions, and it would be misleading to include them here. Hoppers, emergers and raiders are all that you need, coupled, of course, with the Shipman's-style buzzers, which are virtually impossible to improve.

Wrong: *Emerger sitting too high on the water. The unclipped hackle makes the attitude wrong and the fly loses all the silhouette features in the trout's window*

Right: *The clipped hackle lets the fly sit well down in the film. The outline of the fly, particularly the wing, looks good in the window*

Right: Nigel Jackson stocks the 'record' brown at Dever

I believe that we still have a long way to go before we get anywhere near to perfecting the art of the stillwater dries. Nearly all the flies that we currently use, from Shipman's-style buzzers through to emergers and hoppers seem to fall into the suggestive rather than the imitative category. This is best proved by the fact that a small hopper will catch fish when either midge or sedge are on the surface, and that emergers work at virtually any time. In no way is this meant to denigrate those patterns – far from it – but merely to point out that few, if any, of them could be described as being 'close copy'. When we look at the huge lengths to which river anglers will go to get exact copies of hatching flies, with olives in every colour nuance, then it seems to suggest that we could develop some closer copy patterns for the principal lake insects. After all, you need a fair degree of artistic licence to relate the amber hopper to a crane fly, or a red Shipman's to a large red midge.

It could be, of course, that we don't actually need these close copies. The current crop of patterns work very well, and the situation may compare to the all-time greats like the Invicta: the latter is said to suggest the confused outline of hatching midge or sedge, without directly imitating either. The proof of the pudding is in the catching, and there is a special quality about the Invicta that sets it apart. In the same way it could be that the hoppers have been developed as far as is necessary and that current patterns will last for many generations. Equally, the next and crucial stage of their development could be just around the corner, which is exactly what keeps me, and hundreds of other tyers, glued to the bench.

Throughout every winter, and on occasions during the season, I play around with new or experimental tyings. This could be on nothing more than a whim or fancy, or it could be that some weird and wonderful tying material has come my way. The products of these sessions are often discarded as failures, but occasionally they throw up something useful. In 1991, it produced something very useful indeed – a new family of flies that I have called (in the absence of any other inspiration) the shell-back emergers. They enjoyed very positive success all through the year, frequently out-fishing the more conventional emergers, and they have worked in a variety of colours. Perhaps more than anything else, they 'look' right – a factor that has always been important to me in my fishing career.

Until that time, virtually all my emergers were tied or designed with one factor as paramount: silhouette. I believe that this is more important than shape, size and colour – probably more important than all three factors put together. The new 'shell-backs', as they have been christened, still concentrate on silhouette, but also introduce an added element of flash and life to the dressing. The addition of the shell back could be said to suggest the shuck or case of the emerging insect, or equally the little gas bubble that builds up when the fly is at the stage of eclosion. As ever, the technical reasoning is relatively unimportant, and what really matters is how the pattern fishes. In the case of the shell backs, they fish very well indeed.

The material in question is called Spectraflash, and it originates from West

Top left: *State of the art fly tying from Kent Bullfinch. Picture courtesy of Gamefishing Publications Ltd*

Top right: *Too pretty to kill - the stamp of a fish that demands Catch-and-Release*

A good Chew fish comes to the net

A simple buzzer pattern. Note the use of the special shaped hook, which adds life to the fly.

Germany from a company called Traun River Products. It has many uses and I suspect that it will shortly be widely available. It comes in sheet form, with a pearly effect on one side and a 'matt' insect/pearly colour on the other. To make the shell back you simply cut a small piece of material, in an elongated oval shape about 1in long and ¼in at the widest point, and tie it in as you would a normal wing-case. The sparse hackle is then tied in ahead of this. The full dressing could not be easier:

Hook: Partridge Captain Hamilton dry fly, sizes 12–14
Body: Blended amber seal's fur
Shell back: Spectraflash
Rib: Fine gold wire (taken over the entire body, including the shell back)
Hackle: Two turns honey cock hackle

The shell backs have been among my most successful 'new' flies of recent years and they are best tied in amber, claret or red (scarlet). Despite the fact that there are so many green midge around on so many reservoirs, the green and olive shell backs are not nearly so good. If nothing else, this proves again the fickle nature of fishing, or maybe just Sod's Law was actually invented by an angler!

Winged emerger   *Shell-back emerger*

Two interpretations on the same theme. On both flies, the underneath of the hackle has been clipped to help the fly sit well down in the surface film. This clipping should be done in line with the underbody of the fly

DRY FLY RULES

The following paragraphs contain comments that are fundamental to successful dry-fly fishing. Some may seem obvious, yet it is surprising how often they are overlooked or even ignored.

To begin this section, there are two very different ways of casting at a moving fish. Let us assume for a moment that we are fishing the dries from a boat and that the fish are moving upwind towards us.

Forward Lead

In virtually every circumstance, you will need to incorporate a degree of 'forward lead' in the cast. In other words, you will be looking to lay the flies ahead of his last-known position (rise or sighting) so that he moves on to them. This forward lead needs to be adjusted for both the speed of the boat's drift, and also for the speed of the fish. The general rule is that if you are in doubt, it is better to give too much forward lead rather than too little; the latter carries a high risk of spooking the fish or even of landing the flies right on top of him.

A three-pounder goes back at Chew

A take on the lift-off at Grafham

Forward lead is easier to predict if there is some angle to the cast, as opposed to a cast straight down the line of the drift. It is for this reason that most dry-fly experts will always insist on 'working the angles' by varying their casts. Indeed, many of them will select a fish that is to the side of the boat rather than one which is 'down the line'. Remember that in loch style fishing both anglers effectively have 90° of angle available to them, and providing you co-ordinate your casting with your boat partner, it is perfectly possible and practical to cast at right angles to the line of drift.

It has to be said that some of the hardest fish to catch on dry fly are the ones that come directly towards you, allowing no angle at all in the cast. Forward lead is still required, but it is harder to gauge, especially as you will have to 'stop' the line as it unfurls in order to get good turnover and presentation. Such presentation is still needed on an angled cast, as is the stopping of the line, but it is noticeably harder to assess the exact range for a down-the-line cast. Not only that, but the fish has less chance of seeing the fly or flies if they are in line ahead of him, whereas an angled cast gives the angler the luxury of three flies across his line of travel.

Point of Contact

A great deal of nonsense is talked about how to strike into a fish. The old myths about saying a mental 'one, two, three' are totally out of place, as are the over-long pauses expounded by some 'experts'. The truth is that each fish is different and each fish will react differently as he takes the fly. The only rule about striking with the dries is that there are no rules.

The essence of stillwater dry fly is that everything is so visual, and this applies especially to the point of contact. You will see everything that you need to see, and the bit that really matters is when the fish actually closes his mouth on the fly. Once the mouth is closed, then any strike will take a hook-hold. The most common mistake that is made is to strike at the rise rather than at the point of contact, an understandable error given the excitement of the circumstances. It is all too easy to take the fly away before the fish has actually taken it, or to pull it from a mouth that is still open. Consequently, if we are looking for a rule-of-thumb, it is fair to say that a slightly late strike is better than an early one.

For me the point of contact represents everything that dry-fly fishing is about. I watch for the moment that the fish comes to the fly and try to gauge when he has it in his mouth. Sometimes this is obvious: a good roll-over, with head, back and tail coming out of the water, leaves little doubt when the fly is taken, as invariably you can actually see the jaws close. For the less obvious takes, the sips or even the sub-surface takes if the flies are somewhat drowned, require intense observation. Again, if in doubt you should leave the strike a touch late.

Fish moving across the flies can always be struck with confidence, as a scissor hook-hold is assured. Fish travelling 'up the line' need more care and consequently a little more time. Two seconds may seem like an eternity in fishing, but that is the absolute maximum that I would allow for a strike. Any longer and the fish will almost certainly reject the flies.

The point of contact can vary. From the above it will seem that it can be virtually instant for a good head-and-tail, to around two seconds at most. Any longer is far too risky.

Laying an Ambush

This is an alternative method of presenting the dries to a moving fish. It could be said that it is little more than an extension of the forward lead rule, but in practice it has so much to recommend it that I feel it deserves a separate designation.

As the name implies, you are effectively laying an ambush for the moving fish by placing the flies in his line of travel. Where this differs from the forward lead technique is that you cast much further ahead and take a lot longer over preparing for the fish's arrival at the crucial point. The extra time enables you to take a few pulls on the line to straighten the leader and to ensure that the leader has sunk. It also means that you have extra time to ensure that the fish is still on line – if not, you can lift off and cast again.

Most important of all, using the ambush method means that any disturbance on the water as the line and leader lands is kept well away from the fish. If they are being fussy, or if conditions are near calm, then this lack of disturbance can be critical; they will now approach the flies confidently, instead of with a degree of suspicion if they have felt the line landing.

When bank fishing the dries, you obviously have a much firmer 'platform' for the cast and also more thinking time. For this reason it is practical to opt for the longer forward lead cast at a moving fish. Because the speed of such fish is variable, it is not possible to give any meaningful distances here. However, assuming that the fish is head-and-tailing in 'typical' fashion, then the flies should be laid in the water at least 8–9 ft in front of the last rise.

Floatant

One of the best products to reach the market for many years is Gink, the only floatant you will need. It is easier to use, less messy and more economical than all the sprays and gels that preceded it. Having said that, the application of floatant is an area where there appears to be some confusion, so it is worth a word of clarification.

Most people apply far too much Gink to their flies, which actually defeats the object. It must be applied sparingly – too little is better than too much. In warm weather, when Gink is more liquid than gel, it is enough just to wet the forefinger and thumb and tease this into the fly. In colder conditions, when the substance is quite thick, just warm a tiny spot of Gink between your fingers and this will make it easier to apply. Never apply Gink directly onto the fly as this will clog the hackle fibres and ruin the presentation. It is also vital to avoid getting any floatant on the leader, particularly those few inches near to the fly itself. Remember, we want the fly to float, but the leader to sink.

Some flies, particularly the larger sizes of hopper or the raider patterns, will benefit from a light pre-Gink at the tying bench as this allows time for the floatant to really to work itself into the body of the fly. For smaller and slimmer flies, just one application at the waterside is sufficient.

Re-Ginking

There will sometimes be a need to re-Gink the flies during fishing. After prolonged use of a fly or team of flies, the floatant gets washed away and the flies will sink. In such instances it is far better to dry the flies in a towel or cloth before the re-Gink, as this enables the Gink to 'take' properly. There is an excellent product on the market from Orvis called 'Dry 'n Float' which consists of a compound of dry crystals that are dusted into the fly, completely drying it out. A very light re-Gink is then all that is needed.

'Drying Casts'

In normal conditions, there is little need for a re-Gink and a few 'drying casts' are all that will be needed. This is achieved by just a few air-casts, snatching hard at the forward stroke as if you were trying to whip the line. This expels the water from the flies very effectively, and is more practical and less time-consuming than a re-Gink. Be careful not to over-extend these drying casts, as line flash can easily spook the fussy fish.

'Pulled' Dries

It may seem that there is a huge gulf between pulling tactics and fishing the dries, but in fact there can sometimes be a direct link. In certain conditions it is quite possible, or indeed very necessary, to 'pull' the dries to provoke a reaction from the fish.

On many occasions in recent years I have been fishing dries to moving fish, but with little or no reaction. Everything seems to be right, with spot-on casting and presentation, but the fish either turn away or ignore the offering at the last moment. I first 'discovered' the effectiveness of the pulled hopper by accident: I had made a long cast at a rising fish but he changed direction as the flies hit the water, so I started to strip them in to recast. To my great surprise, the fish immediately detoured from his former leisurely feeding path and came bow-waving after them, just as if I was stripping a couple of Soldier Palmers in a big wave. He hit the hopper with total confidence, as though it was the one fly he had been waiting for all morning.

Since that time I have frequently tried pulled dries, with varying degrees of success. There seems to be no set pattern to it and no fixed conditions when it is right to pull. It therefore becomes a matter of trial and error, although as a rule-of-thumb I will generally try pulling any dries I happen to be fishing at least once in every half-hour. It is very much a case of options, with a potential of the best of both worlds.

Stalking

For me, one of the best forms of dry-fly fishing is stalking, and this is not, as the name might imply, a tactic that is restricted to bank fishing. While it is obviously possible to stalk a rising fish from the bank, with the attendant need for stealth and concealment, it is more exciting to do the same thing in a boat.

By definition, you naturally have to be able to see the fish that you are stalking, so this method is best in a near or flat calm. In such conditions the fish tend to move in a more haphazard fashion, with less of the directional rises that they make in a rise or ripple. It is not uncommon to see them rising in circles or criss-crossing a small area where there may be a localised insect hatch. If this can be spotted, then the boat can be slowly and above all quietly moved into position on the oars. With the help of a good boat partner, you can often stalk or follow the same fish for a quarter of an hour or more, providing that you are quiet in the boat and that you take careful strokes with the oars.

In these circumstances, it is best to take as long a cast as possible at the fish. Taking him at maximum range reduces disturbance and usually results in a confident take. On the other hand, do not be tempted into making the cast too soon or at such a range that you have to over-extend your cast, as this carries the real risk of sloppy and brutal presentation. As ever, it is a case of sensible and realistic compromise.

Use of the Oars

This probably sounds obvious, yet it is surprising to see how many anglers still use the boat's engine for even the smallest change of position. It is far better to use the oars: there is less disturbance (for you and others) and there is less chance of the boat running on and over-shooting your chosen spot. This has particular application to those times when you need to move the boat about 20 yd or so, to intercept a fish that is moving out of range.

Location

Successful stillwater dry-fly fishing is all about a combination of factors and a blending of many different techniques. Because it is so essentially visual, it has a high entertainment value and it is very easy to become totally preoccupied with it as a fishing style. Many anglers now tackle up with a slightly blinkered approach of declaring that they are going to be 'on the dries' all day. They get out on the water, see that nothing is moving and are left floundering. This raises two points, and both are concerned with attitude rather than any specific tactic: first, never go out on the water with preconceived notions as to what the day will bring. All too often they will be wrong, and a blank day on the dries, no matter how nice a style it is to fish, is still a blank.

The second point is about location, or choice of spot, and this is probably more relevant to dries than to any other method. Most larger stillwaters need to be

Rutland Water: superbly maintained boats, and top-class water management

regarded not simply as one vast expanse of water, but rather as a collection of waters. They will all have areas of contrasting depths, contour and character, but more importantly they have areas of differing fly life. The potential for insect activity is most definitely not the same for the whole lake; witness the number of times we can identify localised hatches and it follows that we should examine the possibilities in every part of the water before we venture out.

As an example, let us say that we are planning a boat day in June on Rutland and that we are looking for areas where we might be able to fish the dries. In view of the great depths (which are identifiable on the contour maps as with most fishing lodges) we are unlikely to see much activity in the main bowl area or in the deeper part of the arms. We will be much better off looking in the tops of the North or South Arms, preferable near any water inlets, or in areas of known shallow water such as the Bunds or Lax Hill. This rather over-simple summary does at least reduce the planned fishing area from 3,500 acres down to around 500, and on smaller lakes it can be fine-tuned to a much greater degree.

The same is true of the location of preferred insect habitat. Midge hatches are likely to occur over a silty bottom, especially near inlet streams, and sedges are likely to be found on stony ground or near walls and dams. In September the crane flies are likely to be blown onto the water by the wind and fish will naturally move upwind and stay near the bank to intercept them. The main point is that there is more to choosing your best spot than mere chance.

And finally...

It is difficult to write this section on dry fly without injecting an excess of enthusiasm into the pages. Like many of my contemporaries, I am unashamedly hooked on the dries and I frequently fish them even if I know that there is only scant chance of success, and at times when I know that I should be doing something else. Like everything else in fishing, it is a matter for some subjective choice. One thing is sure, however, and that is that dry-fly fishing is supremely pleasurable and relaxing, while at the same time being intensely visual and exciting. What more could we ask?

Pulling Tactics

THE ONLY TROUBLE WITH fishing the dries on stillwater is that it is too pleasurable. It is all too easy to get locked in to the method, to the exclusion of all else. If it is not held in check, it can reach the stage where you tackle up automatically with the dries, ignoring all the other possibilities and regardless of the weather or other conditions. It is a marvellous way of fishing, but it can lead to a blinkered approach if you aren't careful. Flexibility of approach is still vital, even on seemingly perfect days.

In the warm summers of 1989 and 1990, when use of the dries was so much the vogue method, it seemed that the majority of anglers had virtually forgotten about pulling tactics. It was viewed with more than a little disdain, and was only considered when conditions for the dries were totally impossible. All that changed with the indifferent weather of 1991, which was a year when many anglers rediscovered pulling tactics; it was also a year when even the classic top-of-the-water fisheries such as Chew were out of sorts, and a combination of weather and water conditions meant that the trout's feeding patterns changed. In general terms they fed in deeper water, taking huge numbers of small midge, preferring to feed at depths of 4ft or more rather than on the surface.

Thus it was that the 1991 season saw a return to prominence of pulling methods and a re-establishment of a more measured and flexible approach. More than anything, it underlined the need for a complete armoury of methods, with sunk line, pulling and dries all given equal consideration.

For myself, I have always enjoyed pulling, particularly with the floating line. It is very much the 'traditional' method, and while there are the national variations such as the Irish short-line style, or the Bristol long-liners (to cite the two extremes), we are still talking essentially about the same thing: the relatively straightforward cast-and-retrieve of a team of flies either in front of a drifting boat or from the bank. Pulling with sinking lines of varying densities is covered in a later section, allowing us for the moment to concentrate on the floaters.

Bill Field with a winning basket from Chew

Stony walls are ideal stock fish habitat, as well as good sedge country

BANK PULLING

In general, pulling tactics are likely to be associated with boat rather than bank fishing. Nevertheless, it is possible to adapt almost all the boat-fishing methods outlined in this book to bank situations, which is why I have purposely avoided making any clear-cut distinctions between the two disciplines wherever possible.

Pulling implies a certain speed of retrieve, which I suppose is normally matched up to the drift-speed of the boat, so bank pulling is necessarily a more relaxed affair. In most bank-fishing situations on large stillwaters I prefer to fish with the wind on either shoulder rather than from behind or in my face. This permits cross-wind casting and the all-important drift-round of the flies as the wind and wave gives extra life to the retrieve. Unless there are known concentrations of food items such as daphnia, likely on downwind banks, bays, corners or dam walls, I will opt for a bank where a typical cast of 90° finishes at about 45° at the end of the retrieve.

Fly patterns are much the same as for the boats, although pupae and nymph are more likely to be favoured in lieu of traditionals and palmers. In essence, pulling on the bank is slower and more controlled.

More than anything on the bank, I like to be mobile. Rarely will I subscribe to the 'static angler' syndrome that is all too prevalent on most waters. We have all seen them: they arrive before dawn, plant the landing net more as a 'keep-off' sign than as an aid to landing fish, and refuse to budge all day. They haughtily leave the water on the odd occasion, arguably to rest the swim, but apart from that they are fishing the same arc of lake for the duration. Regrettably, many such stake-outs are made by inadequate casters, clumsy waders or even fishmongers. The only policy is to leave them to it and to find another stretch of bank.

The only time when the stake-out has any justification is in the evening, when there can be merit in wading into position and then standing on the spot for minimal disturbance as the fish move in to the margins. Even then I still like to move around a little, perhaps stalking an individual fish or exploring different parts of the bank. In the daytime this is always the case and I will think nothing of fishing half a mile or more of bank during a morning, prospecting with a cast here and there. Most reservoirs have fair variety on their banks, and monotonous fishing in only one spot will soon create an exclusion zone of around 30yd from any angler. Fish learn very fast, and even on opening day it takes only a few hours for them to realise that they are a lot safer if they stay just beyond casting range.

In terms of bank fishing, it is hard to say where pulling ends and nymphing begins, or indeed if there is any need for such lines to be drawn. Bank anglers generally need to be more aware of watercraft than their boat counterparts and to be alert to all the happenings in and on the water. It is primarily about a slow, measured approach; in the boats, everything is moving – the angler, the boat, the water and the fish. On the bank, the angler is static and the tactics are adjusted accordingly.

BOAT PULLING

Traditional loch style is most people's conception of pulling a floating line in a boat. With a good ripple on the water, and certainly when it gets too rough for realistic dry-fly work, then most of us reach for the pulling flies.

To the long list of traditional wet-fly patterns we can add the classics of Bibio, Grenadier and the myriad of palmered flies. My favourites are listed at the end of the book, but it would be impossible to list all the variations that exist on themes of flies like the Soldier Palmer. A few years ago it was very much a case of being spoiled for choice, as I had Soldier variations for nearly every reservoir in the country. I also like to pull nymphs on occasion, with a larger fly on the point position to help balance the team of three. This might be a size 10 Pheasant Tail, or an Ombudsman, or my favourite Green Tag Stick which is one of the best pulling flies of all time. The brighter attractors also have their place on a pulled floater, with the Peach Doll being one of the few patterns that falls outside my natural food philosophy, but these are normally reserved for conditions of murky water. The really bright mini attractors are more likely to score when pulled on sinking lines and will seldom feature on my floating line team.

The long line versus short line argument has been raging for many years and I cannot recall hearing a more ludicrous debate. Surely your persuasion is of no importance provided that you enjoy your chosen method? Personally, I favour the supreme versatility of the long line, which is often termed 'Bristol style', in that it opens up so many more possibilities. It is inescapable logic that just because you have 30yd of line on the floor of the boat, it does not mean that you have to use it on

A mini-muddler, one of the best pulling flies of all time, with the ability to create a wake as it is retrieved

The Green Tag Stick, tied short for use as a dropper fly

every cast. In the course of any boat-fishing session I will reckon to make casts of every length, from 3 to 33yd, and I like the potential to cover a fish at maximum range if the opportunity presents itself.

Like most long liners, I also prefer to cover a fish at the earliest possible moment. The further he is from the boat the less chance there is of him being spooked by noise or vibration and the less chance he has of seeing you or the line or rod flash. It is also a fact that accurate casting and good presentation are easier to achieve at a range of 15–20yd than they are close in. Link this with the fact that if you make a mistake with the cast at 20yd there is still the chance of a 'second shot', and you have a fairly sound case for long lining or at the very least the need for some flexibility in a short line approach.

Everything that was said about forward lead and ambush laying in the dry-fly section has equal relevance to pulling. Whether you are fishing to seen fish or simply pulling blind through heavy waves, cross-casting (using all the available angles) is good policy. Most pulling flies look better when viewed from the side than they do stern on, and if the fish misses one of the team there is still the likelihood of him seeing another. A monotonous downwind cast-and-retrieve pattern is just that – monotonous. Exploring all the angles demands concentration, keeps you alert and varies the presentation.

If there is a choice, I will always opt for the stern position in the boat. This is partly because I am more comfortable at that end (and I seldom trust boat partners to keep their flies out of my hat in a big wind), but it is also because I find I can cover more angles. I should stress that this is a personal preference, as many of my colleagues on the competition circuit favour the bows. There is also little doubt that when fishing the sinking line there are marked advantages in the bow spot, as it is possible to work or hang the line right around the bow drift. The spirit of boat fishing, and indeed the international rules, allow for the two anglers in the boat to have an equal share of the 180° angle available. In practice, it is either impractical or impossible for the bow man to fully explore his 90°, whereas the man in the stern has no such restrictions. Provided that both anglers know what they are doing and are prepared to stagger the casting, there should be no problems. But the man in the stern will be more comfortable.

In any pulling situation, it is important to be alert to any change in the feeding depth of the fish. Obviously, when fish are showing at the surface in any degree there can be little question that the flies should join them there. Even so, in a big wave these same fish may well be holding or cruising at a few feet or more and taking wave-tumbled food items at that depth. We frequently find when pulling floaters that there is a lot of action to the flies, even though very few fish are actually seen. This can be a time for a team of pulling flies tied on heavy-gauge wire hooks to take them just below the waves, working on the reverse of the light wire principle for dry-fly hooks.

In light wave or light ripple, it is possible to use these same heavy hook wires to pull flies at 4–5ft, while still maintaining all the benefits of the floating line. On the bank, and in conjunction with artificially weighted flies, it is feasible to fish flies at 10ft or more with the floater, but this is generally not practical in the boat. Apart from the fact that weighted flies are prohibited in international rules, there is a loss of contact and control at such depths. If conditions demand that the flies are pre-

John Lindsay with a marvellous lake Rainbow in New Zealand

sented at depths beyond 6ft, then I would generally switch to the intermediate line. Even in a flat calm there is always an element of drift to the boat and in the time taken for the flies to reach a working depth there is bound to be an element of 'bow' in the line: such a bow means loss of feel and contact. Leader diameters are a matter of choice, and should in any event be geared to prevailing conditions. However my pulling rig, like almost all my fishing, centres upon lighter line than would be considered 'normal'. Unless there are very particular reasons to the contrary, I will happily fish 5lb Super Strength in all pulling conditions, or even 6lb in a wave. I used to favour staggered leaders, with a progressively decreasing breaking strain, but in recent years I find that these are an unnecessary luxury. My dropper lengths have increased a little over the last couple of seasons, I think with a marginal improvement in results. They are now typically at six inches – noticeably shorter than those in use for dry fly. The basic pulling rig looks like this:

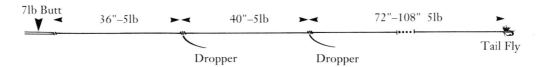

The proportion remains exactly the same if the diameter is scaled up or down, although for leaders of 4lb b.s. or below it is advisable to shorten the tail fly length to a maximum of 84in. With the very light leaders, turnover becomes increasingly difficult, and leaders of below 4lb are very much for fussy fish rather than for general use.

The best advice on leader construction is to use the longest leader with which you can feel comfortable, and that you can consistently cast without tangling. My permanent butt rig involves a section of braided leader into which is spliced a length 7lb standard strength mono:

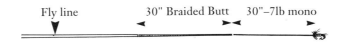

Fly line   30" Braided Butt   30"–7lb mono

This is a fixed rig, onto which all day-to-day leaders are tied. Thus my typical leader will be between 17 and 20 feet overall, with the tail fly section being lengthened either for a heavier point fly, or for really difficult fish. Again, the tail fly length can be anything that you can comfortably cast, and the over-long tail section will give a lovely swim or flow to the tail fly. It also takes the fly as far away as possible from any potential disturbance of line and butt, which is a further advantage on tough days.

Good presentation comes from good turnover, and the gradual tapering of the braided butt smoothes the transition from fly line to leader. These formats also balance in particularly well with the AFTM 5 or 6 line weights, enabling long leaders to be used with comparative ease. The old-fashioned and out-moded idea of simply tying on the team of pulling flies at 3ft intervals is totally wrong. I also know that some anglers favour a four-fly team, but this rarely fits in comfortably with the lighter AFTM line weights and a four-fly bird's nest takes longer to unravel than one with only three flies. Three-turn water knots, or the so-called 'quick' two-turn water knot, are used in all cases.

Just as there are times with the sinking line when the benefits of super-strength nylon are negated, the same is true when pulling the floater. In heavy algae blooms, in muddy or cloudy water, or in a really heavy wave there is no point in using ultra-fine diameters. At times like these it is better to use conventional monofilament, probably in breaking strain of 5 or even 6lb. The reason is that the extra diameter means that the mono is somewhat stiffer and less prone to tangle, as well as having the inherent strength of the increased physical diameter.

On hard days, I have to confess to being an advocate of the 'percentage' approach to pulling. Unlike some experts who suggest teams of either three traditionals or three palmers for the cast, I like to pull with a more varied team. Typically, this will consist of a nymph on the point, a winged traditional in the middle, and either a palmer or perhaps a buzzer on the top dropper. This covers all the percentages, and on a day when there is little or no evidence of available food items it is a good hedged bet. Once that all-important first fish is in the boat, the marrow scoop can reveal all.

With regard to the point of contact, similar rules apply to pulling that were outlined for dry-fly work, except that there is rarely the visual element to assist us. When we can see it all happen, on those heart-stopping moments when a bow-waving fish turns on the fly at high speed, contact is generally made for us and there is nothing to do but control our reactions – don't strike. A simple tightening of the line is enough – sometimes too much – and if possible this is a case for what I call the 'left-hand strike'.

Most people pull flies through one or more fingers of their rod hand, both for control of the line and for sensitivity. However, the problem arises in that the natural reaction is to trap the line at the point of contact and make this a part of the strike. This is fine in some circumstances and can even be obligatory on others, but when you are pulling at speed and a bow-waver decides to have a go, it can lead to disaster. For these takes it is better to release the finger hold altogether and to cushion the strike with a little 'give' from the retrieve hand. In this way it is possible to give a little line at the point of contact and to allow the full flex of the rod to cushion things at the business end.

The left-hand strike is also very useful when dibbling the pulled flies near to the boat. At the moment of the dibble there is relatively little line out and a savage take can result in broken leaders. So when I am dibbling I always release line from the control finger and hold it in the left hand, ready to give line as required.

Much of your strike technique in pulling is determined by the style of fly line that you favour. If you like the low or non-stretch lines, you will enjoy a much sharper and more instant contact with the fish. Indeed, with these lines there is rarely a call for a strike at all, but merely a tightening of the line. Plastic (PVC) lines, on the other hand, can have a lot of stretch to them, particularly when lifting into a fish at maximum range and a positive strike is needed.

Adult grouse wing sedge

For a rule-of-thumb, I would commend the left-hand strike for most circumstances. When it is coupled with a rod-arm lift (to enhance the cushion) it quickly becomes second nature and it is a very flexible way of making contact with even the liveliest of fish.

Sinking-line Tactics

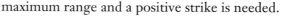

IF SOMEONE HAD TOLD me about ten years ago that I would be writing anything about sinking lines or sinking-line tactics, I would probably have given them a pitying look and then changed the subject. Like most of my contemporaries, I was firmly locked in to using the floater and tended to regard anything other than an occasional intermediate as 'not quite fishing'.

How times change and how quickly has that particular wheel turned full circle. Stillwater trout fishing is moving forward at such a pace that there is no longer any room for a blinkered approach or for any of the misplaced purism that pervaded the sport in the last generation. Fresh ideas, many enquiring minds and an increasingly Hi-tech tackle trade have combined to bring flyfishing well and truly into the twentieth century, and for most of the time these changes have given us a healthier sport.

The reason that I came to the joys of the sinking line so late in life had more to do with geography than anything else. When you live on the banks of Chew and Blagdon, probably the finest top-of-the-water fisheries in Britain, if not in the world,

Top left: *Superb Brownies
like this are a hallmark of
New Zealand, and they love
English tactics*

Top right: *Tony Pawson
OBE – one of fishing's
all-time greats*

*The V1, a Soldier Palmer
variation that has taken
fish all over Britain and
the world*

then you are unlikely to be baptised with anything other than a floating line. Despite all the rewarding nuances of sub-surface tactics, there is still nothing that can compare with the sight of a fish bow-waving after a Soldier Palmer, or the glorious moment when the jaws close on a floating hopper. Such moments still represent the cream of stillwater flyfishing and it is hardly surprising that many Bristol-based anglers never bother to look any further.

But as my angling footsteps became increasingly wider in the mid-1980s, I became aware of another school of thought. It was largely Midlands based and centred upon those two paragon fisheries of Rutland and Grafham. Just as the Bristol philosophy was essentially floating line, the Midlanders had worked out an equally successful way of extracting trout from the water using a sinker, and most of them seemed to be using very fast sinkers. People like Bob Draper were winning every competition that they entered, and because of this very obvious and high profile success others began to take note. Slowly, and after not a few false starts, I was inducted into the use of the sinker. At first it seemed alien and foreign to all my Bristol school of teaching, but gradually it dawned upon me that here was a method that could take a trout when the floater failed. There was, in fact, life after the floating line, and a thoroughly enjoyable and fascinating life it turned out to be.

There followed an intense learning curve when I, and many others like me found out about sinkers. The fastest sinking line in those days was the Hi-D, and it was this line that scored so well for the England team in the 1987 Worldfly Fishing Championships. A cold May and water that had barely warmed above March levels kept every fish in Grafham hard on the bottom, yet I was able to extract them with relative ease with the Hi-D. Other England team members did likewise, and the rest is history.

From that year on, I set about learning everything that I could about sinkers. My armoury of lines had increased from just two – floater and Hi-D – to include two different intermediates, slow-sink, medium-sink and fast-sinking lines, all of which have their place in varying water conditions and depths. I was introduced to such tactics as hold-and-draw, on the hang and the elusive sub-surface dibbling. The concept of induced take was quickly transferred from a chalkstream-only vocabulary, and was found to be just as effective on the lakes. In that same year of 1987 I found myself on that mighty water, Loch Leven, for the autumn international. Any thoughts of floating lines were quickly dispelled by cold winds and a decidedly wintry feel to the weather, and it was only thanks to the fast-sinking line that I gained my heart's desire in the form of the Brown Bowl for the heaviest bag. In that one short but crowded year, my ideas about flyfishing had been changed for ever.

To bring things up to date and to preface the discussion on modern sinking-line tactics, tribute needs to be paid to the fishing-tackle trade. Indeed, it would be impossible to write this without mentioning brand names as they have become a generic reference for the line in question. The tackle that we enjoy today has probably undergone more change in the last twenty years than it did in the last two hundred. As anglers become more sophisticated and more demanding, so the manufacturers have responded in giving us an infinitely better product. It is a far cry from the silk lines of the 1950s and 1960s, with all the attendant mess and preparation, to the super-slick plastics and synthetics that we have now. Yet some things have not changed, as the new non-stretch or low stretch lines are very similar in character and handling to those much vaunted silks, as we shall see shortly.

To make things clearer and to qualify some of the tactics that I hope to explain, I should say now that I am a total convert of the low- or non-stretch sinking lines. Since the latter part of 1991 I have bought virtually all my sinkers from the Airflo stable and have absolutely no hesitation in stating that this one simple move has vastly improved my fishing. I can now enjoy greater fly control, far greater depth control and infinitely better presentation. To make such such statements out of context is to invite a few raised eyebrows, so a little qualification is needed. That qualification comes in the form of the tactics themselves, coupled with the specific lines used to fish them.

INTERMEDIATES

Sometimes referred to as neutral-density (a misnomer) or ultra-slow sinkers, it does not matter what you call them. They are the slowest sinkers of all and for most of the time they are used for fishing in depths of 1–6ft of water. In calm conditions they can be used, of course, for fishing much deeper, but this is to negate most of their advantages and it is far better to opt for a faster sinking line for such depths.

The intermediate is a marvellous line to use and my favourite is without question the XLS 'glass' line from Airflo. This is transparent and has a superbly slick finish that gives wonderful casting properties. More importantly and here is the first real mention of the hi-tech developments – it sinks in a dead straight line and not belly-first as most standard PVC lines. The advantages are huge: the angler has total control of his fishing depth and no longer has to guess where his flies are. He is also in direct touch with everything that happens at the business end and is able to feel the slightest pluck or touch from the fish. Most important of all, you can fish the flies slowly, which is the essence of intermediate fishing.

Intermediate fishing is more about 'feel' than anything else. For most of the time, whether from bank or boat, we are seeking trout that are very much on the feed, and that are holding a depth of 3–4ft for whatever reason. This might be because of a chill in the wind, or because of the bright sunshine that is keeping them off the top. Fly patterns will revolve around nymphs, or possibly a team of 'pulling' flies such as the traditionals or the smaller attractors. Either way, you will need to reach out for the takes and the extra sensitivity of this line is a real boon.

Good intermediate fishing is all about a varied retrieve. Either the figure-of-eight or the pull-and-pause should be interspersed with little pauses or a varied spell of longer pulls to give extra life to the flies. Fish feeding at these depths will often follow but not take and a long pause of five or six seconds will often provoke them into snapping at the fly. Similarly, the end of the retrieve can be pulled up into a dibble just below the surface, with many takes occurring as the flies actually break through. Again, holding the flies in the surface film for protracted periods can be deadly.

It should be said that not all lines that purport to be intermediates really fall into this category – some are almost fast sinkers. Apart from the Airflo, the only other that I use is the Orvis. This is a good neutral tan colour and actually sinks more slowly than the Airflo. Despite this, its disadvantage is that, like all PVC lines, it sinks belly-first with the resulting lack of control.

SLOW AND MEDIUM SINKERS

It is in this area that the advantages of low- or non-stretch lines really begin to show themselves to the full. For obvious reasons, the visual element is now lost and the angler has to rely almost exclusively on 'feel' and his sense of touch. The PVC lines, with all their stretch, cannot possibly transmit sufficient feel to the hands. Coupled with their universal tendency to sink belly-first, you have at best only a remote contact with the flies. At worst, you will not even feel the takes at all.

I would class the slow to medium sinkers as fishing in depths of 5–10ft of water. They are particularly useful when fishing over such depths, which for most reservoirs or lakes can be termed as being reasonably shallow, but are equally good when fish are holding at these levels, despite the fact that the water is much deeper.

Fly line colour is also a factor here, and I prefer the darker olives or browns for the slow sinkers. Purely on the grounds of its high sensitivity, I now use the Airflo Super+ slow sink, which is a non-stretch line in a blue/green colour. The only alternative is the XLS slow sink, which has a slightly slower sink-rate – an ideal choice when you are trying to locate deep weed-beds or other sub-surface features.

FAST OR SUPER-FAST SINKERS

The advantages of non-stretch lines can be seen to the full in this section. Until recently, people tended to quote 'the Hi-D' as an all-embracing title for fast sinkers, but the problem is that the actual Hi-D has its faults. Because of its density, the belly sinks very much faster than the lighter line at either end. This means that for most of the time you are retrieving a great underwater bow of line. When this is coupled with the high degree of PVC stretch, you are facing a fairly serious loss of sensitivity.

With the non-stretch line – and first choice must be the Airflo Di Line – the line sinks almost in a straight line. This is because modern technology has produced a manufacturing process called 'density compensation' which effectively balances the density in the line, irrespective of how thick it actually is. With this line it is possible to feel the slightest touch from a fish, and because you are in direct contact the strike can be gentle and positive. For most of the time, a gentle lift is all that is needed to hook the fish.

The actual sinking speed of any individual line will vary and the times quoted by the manufacturers have little relevance. For instance, the newness of a line will affect its sink rate, as will the AFTM rating. Most anglers will therefore use the count-down principle for their fast sinkers, allowing so many seconds for the line to reach the desired depth. With fast sinkers, this can be anything from 8ft to about 20ft. Greater depths are possible for the bank angler, but snagging on the retrieve is almost inevitable. For the boat fisherman, the drift of the boat precludes realistic fishing at greater depths. Many anglers think that they are fishing very deep, but in reality their flies are often some 10ft higher in the water. The truth is that density compensated lines, sinking in a straight line, will attain far greater depths than the old belly-first PVC varieties.

A great many nuances of retrieve are possible with a fast sinker. They vary from a straightforward pull-and-pause, through all the combinations of sink-and-draw. Flies can be fished static, on 'the hang', or they can be fished at great speeds, but more than anything it is the depth that is crucial, and it is here that many anglers are either unaware of or oblivious to the central fact of which line to use.

Until recently, one line held sway for fast sink work, the Scientific Anglers Hi-D. It is still a good line, but it does have its faults: it sinks belly-first and for much of the retrieve the angler will be pulling his flies in a great underwater arc. He may think that line and flies have reached fishable depths, but in fact it is only the line that is down there – the flies, leader and several yards of thinner line will be well above. This is hugely important and is the one thing that highlights the benefits of density compensation: the whole line sinks to the required depth, and that is where the flies are fished. For me, the Airflo Di Line, in a dark charcoal-grey colour, is the only line. Coupled with its non-stretch characteristics, it gives unbelievable level of sensitivity when fishing at these depths.

With a level sinking line, the advantages of 'counting down' the line as it sinks are magnified. On a cold day on Rutland, for example, I was able to locate fish feeding at around 12ft, and it took only about ten minutes of experimenting. You start with a ten-second sink time and then increase this to about fifteen seconds, then twenty, and so on. Half-a-dozen casts at each speed are enough and it is a highly effective fish-finding process.

But locating fish at depth is not everything, as you now have to work out the best retrieve pattern for them. Occasionally, it will be enough simply to pull through them, with varying speeds of pull-and-pause. More often, though, fish at depth will be fussy and will need to be teased or tempted into taking, which is the main reason behind the current vogue for the variations on the hold-and-draw theme. For most of these, a long cast of about 25yd is needed. In fact, this represents few problems with the fast-sinking lines and most anglers find that with practice it is possible to cast almost a full line.

It should also be said that these are predominantly boat-fishing tactics. While they are practicable from the bank, there is rarely sufficient depth available to work them properly. I hardly ever use anything faster than a medium-sinker for bank fishing.

From the boat, though, it is a different story. The principle of hold-and-draw is that the line is cast out, allowed to sink to the prescribed depth and then the bulk of it is retrieved. When about 5yd of line remain, the retrieve is stopped dead; the line then continues to sink until it is hanging vertically beneath the boat, from where it is either inched up or teased up until the leader but breaks surface. Then it is held again – a point at which many takes occur – before finally drawing up the cast and lifting off. It will quickly be seen that an infinite number of variations on this theme can be played.

The expression 'on the hang' refers to catching fish with a static retrieve, holding the flies beneath the boat for anything from 5 to 50 seconds. If such a length of time

Battling hard, a big rainbow dives under the boat

sounds fanciful, it is not: I have had fish take after what seems like an age on the hang. With this method, it is possible to tease fish that are holding at depths of some 20ft and you need to imagine them swimming around the flies, undecided at whether or not to take. This is classic induced-take and any extra life imparted to the flies at this stage is likely to be rewarded: some will favour little pulls and tweaks, while others will prefer a longer draw interspersed with a shaking of the rod tip – only experimentation will tell on the day.

Depending on the depth of water being fished, you can fish on the hang from just sub-surface down to 20ft or more. The great thing is that when the takes come they are invariably positive: the fish take and then turn down, hooking themselves in the top of the mouth. They are often so savage that no strike is required at all and a gentle tightening is all that is needed.

The idea of sub-surface 'dibbling' is foreign to some, but with practice it becomes a fascinating method. There is just as much skill involved as in using a floater, perhaps more so in that the only visual element comes from watching the line or leader below the rod tip. Occasionally, and in very clear water, you may see the underwater flash of the fish as it turns on the fly, but more often it is the feel on the line that signifies action. This is yet another benefit of the non-stretch line, with its high sensitivity to the slightest take.

On calmer days, even more possibilities are opened up in terms of the fishing depth available, because it is possible to lengthen the amount of line that is fished on the hang. You should keep in touch with the line by a slow retrieve as it sinks, using both sight and touch to ascertain when it is near-vertical beneath you. In absolute flat calm, this is a way of fishing flies effectively at depths of 30ft or more – something that is otherwise totally impractical from a boat.

Sight and touch are also employed when looking for takes on the hang. Throughout the retrieve you should watch the line, looking for the slightest twitch or tweak that denotes a fish. The critical point is when the top dropper leaves the surface, and this is the point at which most anglers will prolong the hold. Any take is registered by a downward movement of the fly which acts as a bite indicator: the strike is seen long before it is felt at the hand. With a leader length of some 10–14ft between the top dropper and point fly, you are still very much in viable fishing depths.

On the big waters like Rutland and Grafham, where drifts of over 40ft of water are commonplace, this can often be the only effective method of fishing, particularly in times of cold water or adverse weather. Even on shallower lakes it is still effective, as by shortening the length of line on the hang the same results can be achieved.

Flies in use are varied, but by far the most popular are those attractors that are rudely termed 'traffic lights'. These are the competition-legal mini-lures and attractors, usually tied with bright fluorescent bodies or wings and with a lot of marabou in them for life and movement. Top flies are the white, hot orange and pink tadpoles, although they can also be tied with a conventional wing at the head. The bright colours are very effective at depth or in conditions of haze or algae in the water. A note of caution is needed, however, because they can have a scaring effect on the fish in very clear water (Rutland in particular), and a change to more suggestive or imitative flies should be made. Stick Flies tied with hen hackles are useful to keep an element of life in the pattern, but I am also happy to fish a typical pulling team on the hang, with a nice mobile Soldier Palmer or even a buzzer.

Fishing on the hang can be intensely exciting. The flies can be left for what seems an age without movement, and just when you think that nothing is happening, a take will come from nowhere. It needs a degree of sub-surface vision to imagine the fish circling the static fly, as well as a good deal of belief in the method. The latter comes with experience and the first few fish on the method are vital to engender the all-important confidence.

So the truth about sinkers is that they are a far cry form the once-held belief of 'chuck'n chance'. Rather, subtlety is required and a level of skill that dictates much practice. It is often said that the best anglers are those who can develop this 'sub-surface vision' and I would certainly subscribe to this. It is no longer enough to think that if the fish are not showing on top, they are simply not feeding at all. Using a sinker without thought can be dreary and monotonous, but by applying a little sub-surface vision it can be turned into something that is fascinating, absorbing and highly rewarding. When this is matched to the latest technology fly lines, we have an angling style that is very special indeed.

THE TRUTH ABOUT SINKING LINES

Sink rates are often quoted at so many feet or inches per second, but this can vary wildly from line to line. Brand new lines or those with different AFTM ratings will sink at different speeds. When buying a line, it is the density that is most relevant – that is, the density of the line in relation to the water. Lines with a lower density than water will float, while those with a higher density will sink – varying densities for varying sink rates. The diagram below shows typical densities for each category, coupled with the relevant guideline sink rates. Some manufacturers are beginning to quote densities as a more meaningful guide.

	Typical Line Density	*Sink Rates*	
		Inches Per Second	*Seconds Per Metre*
Floaters	0.55 0.93	–	–
Intermediates	1.07 1.14	1.4 1.6	26 27
Slow sinkers	1.18	2.0	22
Medium sinkers	1.35	2.3	17
Fast sinkers	1.7 1.8	3.0	13
Very fast sinkers	2.6	4.0	10
Ultra fast sinkers (750g lines)	3.2	6.5	6

NB Sink rates are affected by other factors, including wave action and water temperature. Keeping tension on the line will reduce the sink rate, while releasing it completely (and the forward drift of the boat) will increase it.

Spooning

FISHING TACKLE THAT CAN be termed 'essential' falls into two categories. The first and more obvious is the 'direct' tackle, comprising rod, reel line and flies. It probably also includes good quality waterproof clothing, although even here an element of subjectivity creeps in. The second category consists of a whole spectrum of delights that can either be viewed as 'essential' or 'optional', depending on your attitude to fishing, current frame of mind or bank balance.

For me, the marrow scoop is such an important item of equipment that I would be tempted to class it in the former category. It is nothing short of vital to my whole philosophy on fishing and it would be inconceivable for me to imagine a day's fishing without it.

You may feel that these are strong statements, but fishing is in many ways a matter of personal preference, and this book is about my personal methods and philosophies, so I make no apology for the apparent dogma. Much of my success in the past has come from an imitative approach – that is to say, from the use of flies that suggest or represent items in the trout's diet. Insects or food items that are plainly visible to the angler will often tell only a part of the story, or in some cases they will give a totally false picture. There may be, for instance, a large fall of terrestrial insects on the water, leading us to think that the fish would feed on them avidly, yet often such apparent bounty is ignored by the fish in favour of a sub-surface food source. What you see is not necessarily always what you get.

Proof-positive of what a fish has been eating comes from the marrow scoop. There is, of course, an element of Catch-22 in this, with the age-old argument that every scoop should be sold with a shotgun – before you can use the scoop you first have to catch a fish, and if you don't know what he's been feeding on how do you know which fly to select? While accepting this, it is still perfectly possible to make a 'best guess' fly selection in almost any angling circumstances, especially in early season or cold weather, and then to fine-tune your fly selection once there is some firm evidence from your first spooning.

Firm and positive evidence is exactly what the marrow scoop provides. It removes all the ifs, buts and maybes, and offers the angler positive and irrefutable evidence of what the fish has been eating prior to its capture. In fact, not only what he has been eating immediately prior to capture but for some hours before as well, as we shall see.

I accept that there is a degree of resistance to the use of the scoop by many anglers. They see it as a messy, protracted and in some ways confusing process, and one from which they draw little benefit. A few of them may well be lure fishers for whom the information on the trout's diet has limited use. However, I suspect that most anglers are put off because they are confused about it: either they don't know how to use the scoop properly or they cannot identify its contents. In either case, it is hardly surprisingly that they draw little benefit from the process.

But a little time and patience spent in learning how to use a scoop correctly, coupled with a little experience and practice in sorting through the food items that are likely to be encountered, will be repaid many times over. The process can indeed be messy and may even appear rather too clinical for some tastes, but once the hurdle of resistance has been crossed, it soon becomes plain sailing, with vast benefits to be reaped.

THE RIGHT TOOL FOR THE JOB

Surprisingly, there is a great variety of scoops on the market, and there are good ones to be sought out and bad ones to be avoided. The logical purchase is the combination of scoop and priest, and these come in many forms. You can choose from either brass or aluminium alloy, or a combination of the two. Despite the extra weight, which can sometimes be a little heavy in the waistcoat pocket, this is still the best choice. You *can* buy a separate scoop in either plastic or alloy, but these are far less popular. The plastic ones also tend to have a major deficiency in that scoop itself is too shallow – in other words, the 'cup' is not deep enough and it removes only a part of the stomach contents, which is very misleading. Personally, I favour the priest combination, with a shortish but deep cup to the scoop end.

USING THE SCOOP

Far too many anglers either fail to use their scoops properly or even misuse them completely. The result is that either they remove only part of the stomach contents or sometimes none at all. Common problems include too shallow an insertion and failure to give the all-important full turn.

The correct way is to hold the fish in one had and insert the scoop into its mouth with the cup facing up. Push it well in until light resistance is felt. In the case of a typical 2lb fish, the length inserted will be about 3½–4in. Do not push the scoop in overly hard or far as this will rupture the stomach and spoil the spooning. Once inserted, give one full turn of the scoop and withdraw it with the cup again facing up. The entire stomach contents will be contained in the cup for inspection. To the uninitiated this sounds rather barbaric, but remember that we are dealing with a dead fish and this is nothing other than a very simple autopsy.

INSPECTION OF THE CONTENTS

This is the point at which many people have a quick glance at the contents, make a summary decision as to their make-up, and then discard them. While I would agree that a quick look is better than no look at all, there is no doubt that a lot of information will be lost or overlooked in this way. If you have gone to the trouble of spooning in the first place, it stands to reason that you should take a few more moments to finish the job properly.

There are essentially two ways to inspect the contents. The first involves 'diluting' them. For this you will need a container such as a white Thermos flask cup or a clear plastic beaker which you fill with about half an inch of water. The contents are emptied into this where they can be teased apart. In fact, they tend to separate very easily, enabling you to identify their make-up. Don't use the same Thermos cup that you use for coffee!

The second method, which I favour, is simply to empty the scoop onto the palm of your hand, and then to poke the items until they are clearly identifiable. After a few moments it will quickly become obvious that one particular item is predominant, and this method takes far less time than the dilution process.

TIMESCALE

Assuming that you have used the scoop properly and have extracted all the contents of the fish's stomach, you will also get some clues as to what he has been feeding on over a period of time. The contents at the back of the scoop will represent the latest meal, while those at the lip will be the food items that are up to several hours old. This is particularly relevant to morning and evening fishing, when trout will often change their diet dramatically, sometimes in the space of half an hour. On evenings at Blagdon I have seen scoops where the back end was packed with sedge, whereas the front end contained exclusively midge pupae. Similarly, there have been mornings on Chew where a veritable buzzer feast has trailed off, leaving the trout mopping up nothing but spent cases – all of this was revealed from the marrow scoop. In general, recent meals tend to look 'fresher', whereas older ones degenerate into an amorphous mass.

SECOND SPOONINGS

Occasionally there will be so much food in the fish's system that a second spooning will be necessary. This can occur when the trout are feeding avidly on a large food item, such as crane fly or mayfly, at which times the expression 'packed to the gills' is an apt one. However, at times like this the evidence of the latest meal is so overwhelmingly obvious that it is rarely relevant to make the second spooning and it becomes a matter of academic interest only.

IDENTIFICATION OF THE CONTENTS

So much for the mechanics of the spooning process, all of which are pretty straightforward. We now come to the more complex part of the process and an area which seems to have been studiously avoided by angling writers over the years: the actual identification of the food items in the stomach contents. It is one thing to be able to spoon a fish correctly, but if you are unable to identify what you are looking at, then you are hardly any better off.

Over the course of the last two seasons I have kept a photographic record of innumerable spoonings, with just his chapter of the book in mind. The reason is that no carefully worded descriptions will help the reader in any way: after all, how do you set about describing a mass of muck with a few legs and wings sticking out of it, all of which is in the same drab brown colour? The answer is the series of photographs that now follows. As far as possible I have taken a representative shot of everything that the angler is likely to encounter in stillwater fishing in Britain. Obviously, it would not be possible to identify every food item as there are occasions when fish eat some very unusual items. For example, in my autopsies over the years I have found cigarette butts, bits of weed, stones, and even once a ring-pull from a metal can, but none of these items can genuinely qualify as being regular food intake.

In a similar vein, I have not photographed one item that you are likely to find on a regular basis – an empty scoop. More often than not you will withdraw the scoop and think that you have done something wrong in the spooning, as there will be nothing in the cup except a little bit of slime, water and maybe the odd strand of weed. In fact, empty or negative spoonings are very common, and although they predominate in the mornings, they can and do occur at any time of the day. Trout come on the

A superbly fit rainbow is returned to fight another day

feed in a haphazard fashion and take no account of the human clock or the permitted fishing hours.

There is no true substitute for experience when it comes to fishing. In time you will come to recognise all the main food items at a glance, and I cannot recommend too strongly that you spoon each and every fish that you keep. In this way the items will become familiar and you will build up a mental library of all the peculiarities in your own region or on your own fishery. What follows is therefore a solid grounding in the use of the marrow scoop and it should form a base on which your own research is developed.

A FINAL WORD

As will be apparent from these photographs, fish can often eat a lot of food in a very short space of time. Equally, they can go for long periods without feeding at all, and this is particularly relevant to prolonged spells of hot weather.

There is also a big difference between general feeding and selective feeding. In the former it will be possible to catch a fish on many different flies, but in the latter the requirement will be for a close copy pattern that either suggests or directly copies the food item in question. At times like this it is very rewarding to withdraw a scoop full of buzzers, many of which are still wriggling, and to be able to tie on a copy in the right size and the right colour. If our investigations lead to success, then surely there is a measure of satisfaction to be gained.

The use of a scoop is increasingly relevant to the supreme challenge in stillwater flyfishing, namely the dry fly. Dry patterns are very much in the process of evolution and tying them demands at least a fairly close copy of the natural. Although many current patterns lean more towards a general shape and silhouette, size is still important. I feel strongly that there will be a move to far more imitative and close-copy dry flies in the coming years.

The conclusion of this chapter comes in the form of a tip. If you should lose or forget your scoop, then all is not lost. In extreme conditions, try breaking off a reed stem or a thick stem of hollow grass. It is not a long-term substitute, but in desperate circumstances it can work as a stop-gap.

Dams and Walls

IT CANNOT BE ARGUED that fishing on the dam wall is the most scenic part of the lake or that there is any great aesthetic pleasure in the surroundings. Dams are not attractive constructions: they are functional and are a necessary evil with which we must live in our stillwater trouting. It must also be said that, like it or not, dams and their accompanying concrete aprons are great fish holding areas, presenting the angler with a unique set of opportunities. Fishing in this area is unlike any other part of the lake and has a challenge all of its own. In fact, if you can ignore the lack of scenic appeal, the dam wall can offer some very productive and interesting fishing indeed.

Before looking at the particular tactics involved, it is worth considering for a moment why the dam can be so productive. This is far more complex than simply having the availability of deep water well within casting range and it involves factors that are seasonably variable such as thermoclines and insect life.

The point about insect life is probably the most significant of all. Stones and/or stone walls are the preferred habitat of the sedges and often the best hatches will come from this area. Even when the insects are not hatching, there will still be an abundance of caddis for the fish to feed on, and imitations like the Stick Fly can be fished slow and deep anywhere near the wall. The same is true in the dam corners: in such places there is generally a good silt build-up, and silt is ideal for midges as they bury into the soft mud to pupate. Third on the list come the daphnia and it is a well-known fact that huge swarms of these little crustaceans can build up on the dam. The reason for this is that they get blown along on the current and then come to an abrupt contact with the wall, rising straight up from the lake-bed. When the prevailing wind is blowing onto the dam, that is where the biggest concentrations of daphnia will be.

In high summer or in any period of prolonged warm weather, all large bodies of water will create thermoclines. These are essentially 'lines' or layers of water of varying temperature and they can be very pronounced – sometimes, if it is calm, there can be a difference of 4–5° in less than a foot of depth. Thermoclines can form even in quite rough water and are the main reason for the aerators that can be seen on most big reservoirs (the correct name for the aerators is 'anti-stratification pumps').

Thermoclines affect both the fish and the fishing in several ways. Blooms of algae can occur in defined strata of water temperature and such blooms can be avoided by

Continued on p104

SPOONING

Captions for following colour section

1 *The marrow scoop priest combination. The hole in the priest head allows secure attachment to jacket or waistcoat. Note the deep but relatively short cup.*

2 *This is the state in which most contents are removed, clogged together in a great mass. They need to be separated for analysis. Boat fishing.*

3 *The same spooning, but spread across the palm of the hand for identification. Clearly the fish has been feeding on crane flies, but note also the black beetle and several midge pupae. The date was September and the fish took an Amber Hopper, fished dry and static, in mid-morning. Subsequent hopper fishing was equally successful, even though most fish were packed to the gills. Despite having apparently gorged themselves, they were still feeding avidly. Note the sedge pupae at the top of the picture.*

4 *This fish took a Shuck Fly, fished dry, at noon in mid-June. Top left of the picture is the 'mass' of an earlier meal, but the latest food items are predominantly empty shuck cases. Bottom right shows a terrestrial insect (house fly) and a small black beetle. There was no visible hatch at the time of capture and the fish showed all the signs of mopping up the shucks. Three more fish were taken on the Shuck Fly, until the rise stopped abruptly at 2pm. Boat fishing.*

5 *A huge quantity of small green midge, extracted from a Chew fish that had been feeding at around 6–8ft down in early July. It was taken on a size 12 green buzzer, fished very slow on a 'glass' intermediate line. Huge numbers of these small midge have been an increasing feature on many stillwaters in recent seasons, encouraging the fish to feed at depth. As the picture shows, they were the exclusive food item. Bank fishing.*

6 *This fish was taken at Rutland in late May, from water about 10ft deep off Lax Hill. The successful fly was a Diawl Bach, size 12, fished 'nymphed' at around 2ft on a floating line.*

Conditions were near flat calm, with only a few fish rising. The picture shows brown midge pupae very clearly, most in pupa form, but also one or two that were hatching. Several of these pupae were still wriggling in the scoop, indicating that the trout were almost certainly taking them on their ascent to the surface. Dry emergers were then fished, but with no success – a return to fishing a team of two dark olive buzzers and a Diawl Bach yielded four more fish. Boat fishing.

7 *A mixed bag, from a Blagdon fish taken at 8am on an August morning on Rugmoor Point. The fish took Stick Fly, weighted, and there was absolutely no clue to any insect activity. Note the single corixa left of centre and the solitary caddis pupa bottom centre. The remainder appears to be partly digested adult midge (sparse numbers) from an early morning feed. There is also a single gull feather bottom right, just to add to the confusion. There is very little to be concluded from this spooning, and in fact I had no more pulls that morning. Bank fishing.*

8 *A clear-cut division of feeding is shown here. Top of the picture is a mass of small snails, whereas in the centre can be seen empty shuck cases of large red midge. The fish took mid-morning on Chew, in July, and fell to a Claret Raider fished dry. Only a few adult red sedge were on the surface, but the fish appeared to be mopping up the big cases avidly. The early hatch had probably taken place before the boats went out, yet strangely there were no adults in the spooning. Conditions were gentle ripple and I was able to lay a dry-fly ambush for two more fish in the following hour, both of which took the Claret Emerger. Spoonings from these fish were identical to this one, indicating that the fish had been preoccupied with the snail during the earlier hatch but had now moved up in the water. Boat fishing.*

Captions continued on page 103

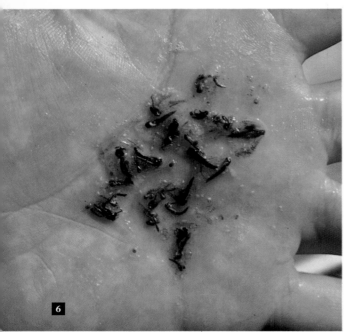

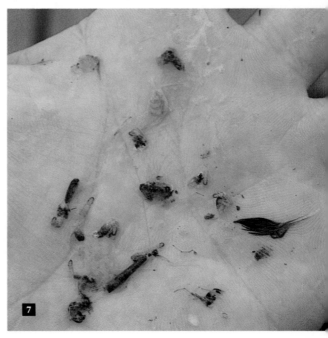

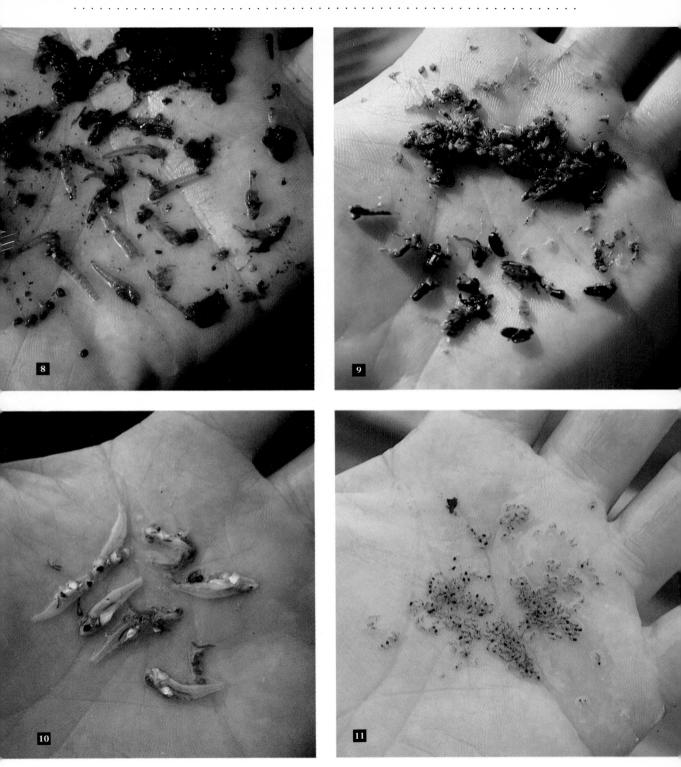

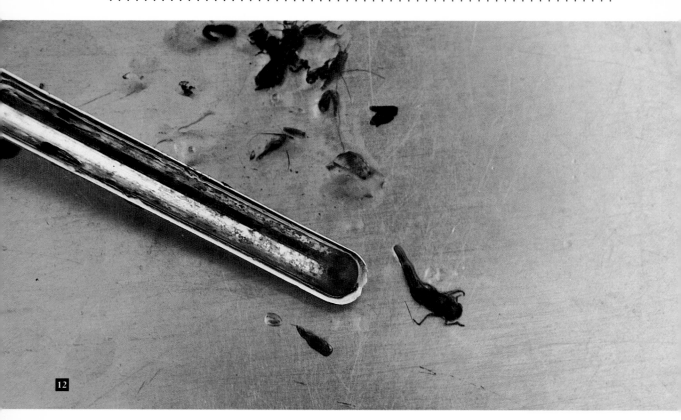

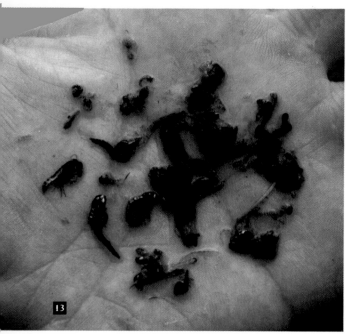

Spooning captions continued

9 *Another mixed bag, with a host of different food items all of which would appear to have been taken in the last hour before capture. The venue was Rutland, fishing in a good off-shore wind at the top of the South Arm. The fish took a Claret Hopper (there is nothing remotely like it in this spooning) fished as a part of a dry-fly team and static, in a fair 6in wave. As well as the packed mass of small green midge, there are several terrestrial insects here, including leaf beetle and small black beetles. There is even a bloodworm in centre shot, as well as a few larger green midge pupae. With such a varied diet and in the near-perfect fishing conditions, it is not surprising that the fish would take almost anything, although relatively few fish were breaking surface. A change to pulling tactics by me and my boat partner provided a dramatic increase in sport, with five fish in the next hour before lunch. Boat fishing.*

10 *The food item here is obvious. The fish was taken from Woodford Bank on Chew, bank fishing over about 10ft of water in early July. Trout were obviously fry feeding and this one fell to a floating fry pattern fished over a bankside weed-bed. Other anglers were having greater success with lures of various sizes and there were fry feeding fish all along the bank. The messy brown items are probably midge pupae, but from a much earlier feeding. Bank fishing.*

11 *The dreaded daphnia. This photograph was taken on opening day at Blagdon (late March) and the fish took a heavy Pheasant Tail fished on an FTA retrieve at around 8ft down on a medium sink line. Absolutely no other food items*

were being taken and none were found in subsequent spoonings through the day. (The black speck top left is just a leaf fragment.) Boat fishing.

12 *Damsel flies are not always the pretty electric blue of the adult. The nymphs are free-swimming and a very drab olive/dark olive colour, and they are more or less the same the world over - this photograph was taken in New Zealand. The lake in question was a mirror image of an English stillwater, with just the same food items as can be seen by the adult midge in the picture. Boat fishing.*

13 *Late September on Chew and a fish that took a dry emerger in very shallow water (4/5ft) in one of the few good buzzer hatches in 1991. The insects were exceptionally large and although my partner and I had been fishing with size 14s a change to 12s and 10s improved our catch rate. Fish were rising very positively (head and tail), although not in great numbers; they appeared to be mostly residential fish, feeding selectively. The picture clearly shows legs on the pupae (extreme left), and pupae, emerging adult and adult were being taken.*

14 *Mostly beyond identification, this mass was from a much earlier meal. There was a mixture of legs and wing-cases, but it was impossible to tell whether they were from midge or sedge. However, it did indicate that the fish had been feeding on top but had withdrawn to some depth, as this one was taken on a slow fished intermediate with weighted nymph (Stick Fly), at around 10ft. The fish took in mid-afternoon and was a one-off – we had no further activity until dusk. Chew, boat fishing.*

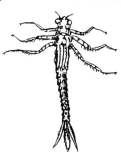

Damsel nymph

the fish. Visibility is drastically reduced and often it will be necessary to use a very bright fly to have any chance of success. In times of heavy blooms, fishing from the dam can have a big advantage, as the angler will be able to fish his flies beneath the coloured strata in the clearer water beneath.

In summer, deeper water is almost always cooler water, which is another advantage of fishing on the dam. Trout will shun warm water and in extremes it can be critical for them and they will retreat to the deeps. For most of the lake banks they will then be inaccessible to anglers, but not on the dam. This is one of the reasons for the frequently heard expression that fish 'patrol' the dam; it is just that they find the two things that they need there – cool water and plenty of food.

Another fact of life that is not always appreciated is that stock fish love dam walls. The reasons for this are open to some debate, but it seems likely that the walls remind them of their previous environment, where they were swimming around in a 'cage' with either well-defined or solid walls. Unlike the resident fish that will hold deeper water, stockies tend to swim much nearer to the surface and are therefore more accessible to the anglers – boat fishermen have known this for years.

So how should we approach dam-wall fishing and what are the most significant seasonal variations to look out for? Are there any special tactics or methods to employ to shorten the odds in our favour?

The answer to these questions needs to be preceded by a word on safety, as dams can be very dangerous places to fish. Any build-up of weed or algae can make the walls slippery and treacherous, so that it is easy for the angler to slip and fall into the water. The shock of cold water, combined with the weight of wet clothes, can make it frighteningly difficult to climb back out, so extreme caution should be exercised. Always wear boots or waders with a good grip on the tread, and take a net or wading stick with you. If possible, fish back from the edge, where the stones are dry. Go on the dam with a friend or companion, so that if the worst happens there will be someone there either to help you out of the water or to raise the alarm.

Dam-wall techniques are in many ways similar to boat fishing: it is not entirely unlike fishing from an anchored boat in that you have a vast range of depth to explore. With bigger fish patrolling deeper water, there is always a better-than-average chance of a specimen, so your tackle should be geared accordingly. For most lines between intermediate and fast sink you can use a shorter leader than normally you would with a floater, with the ideal length at between 12 and 15ft. For single-fly fishing this can be shortened still further, down to around 9–10ft. For boobys or other buoyant flies, leader lengths of 2ft or less will sometimes be required. With the very real chance of a big fish, coupled with the fact that dams are notoriously costly in terms of lost flies, leader strengths of 6lb minimum are recommended.

Fly loss on the dam wall can occur just as easily out of the water as in it, as casting is at best restricted and at worst near-impossible. Most anglers favour a form of 'steeple cast' in this situation as it is the only way of keeping fly and leader away from the stones. Although somewhat restricting in terms of distance, a good steeple cast can easily give 20yd or more, which is perfectly adequate for most waters. Good steeple casting involves throwing the line near vertical on the back cast and then incorporating an element of forward roll on the main casting stroke. It can feel awkward to begin with, but with practice the change in rhythm is easy to achieve.

Stock fish going into the lake cages at Chew. By the time of final release they are fully acclimatised to the water

As will already be apparent, one of the critical aspects of dam-wall fishing is the control of the depth at which the fly performs. This can be achieved in many ways but by far the most common is by using the 'count-down' process. Lines of varying densities have known sink rates and these can be used to give a fairly accurate guess at where the fly is fishing. But even if you do not know these sink rates, it is still perfectly practical to use the count-down method. You simply cast the line out and then count to ten before retrieving. If after half-a-dozen casts there is no response from the fish, try counting for 15 seconds before the retrieve, and so on. Even with a very fast sinking line, it will often be necessary to wait for a minute or more before commencing the retrieve.

Obviously the time needed for the count-down will vary during the season and will be dependent on temperature and water conditions. It is, however, a very effective method of fish-finding. It needs to be combined with the pattern of retrieve in use as it can be difficult to match a very slow retrieve with, say a fast-sinking line. The answer here is to choose a slower sinker and sacrifice the time it takes for the line to sink in favour of a better and more effective retrieve.

A popular mistake when dam fishing is to underestimate how close the fish will come to the sides. Many anglers lift off too early and are in fact missing the most productive yards of the cast. Fish coming from depths will often follow the fly right to the surface before taking, only deciding to take the fly at the point of lift-off.

In general terms, the best fly patterns to use around the dam are those that can be fished slowly. These are the flies with built-in movement, either from materials like marabou or from softer hackles. The Montana nymph is good, as is the aforementioned Stick Fly (Green Tag). 'Slower' nymphs or attractors such as Viva or Olive Tin Heads are also effective, plus, of course, the ever-faithful buzzers and sedge pupae for imitative fishing. Anti-snag loops can be used as shown in the diagram and this can make a real difference to your fly stocks if the walls are particularly rocky.

So ends a brief introduction to dam-wall fishing. It is not the most exotic location on the lake, but given a little thought and preparation it can be one of the most productive. In the height of summer, it may well be the only way of getting amongst the fish.

Normal Stick Fly

'Loop' Stick Fly or 'Pipe Fly'

Anti-snag loop (right), as tied on a Green Tag Stick Fly. This pattern used to be called the 'Pipe Fly' on Chew as it was fished near an underwater outlet pipe that always snagged conventional flies.

Before tying, catch in a length of 4in of 8lb monofilament at the tail. Then tie the fly in the normal way, up to the throat. Before tying the hackle, catch in the mono to form a loop outside of the hook bend. Cut off any excess mono and finish the hackle.

Polaroiding

THERE ARE FEW INSTANCES in life where the dreams of marketing men come true. Such a rarity occurs when a brand name transcends the product to become a generic title, embracing a whole host of other brands of lesser status. Thus we have 'Hoover' when we really mean 'vacuum cleaner' and 'Bacardi' when was actually mean 'white rum'. But the greatest of them all must be 'Polaroids' that all-embracing name that covers many hundreds of polarising sunglasses available all over the world.

Many items of fishing equipment can be regarded as optional, but among the essentials come polarising glasses. Purely on the grounds of safety most anglers will wear them, as they provide an obvious measure of protection from potentially lethal flying hooks. They also offer a degree of sub-surface vision, at varying levels of quality, that is a real bonus to the fishing.

This sub-surface vision is relative to the style of fishing that is being undertaken. It varies from virtually nothing when we are fishing loch style in a big wave through to being absolutely crucial to successful fish location on a clear stream or river. There is, however, one stage further: the rapidly growing band of anglers who enjoy the ultimate challenge in the sport, the careful stalking of individual specimen fish in river, stream or lake. For them, the total one-to-one contact with the fish is everything as it represents and fulfils the true hunting challenge. They will mark down an individual fish and spend hours, perhaps even days, in stalking it. Such anglers are going 'polaroiding'. The original expression was coined in Australia, where polaroiding is the accepted way of fishing. On Tasmania in particular, where the large shallow lakes provide an ideal shoreline habitat for the big brown trout to cruise for food, the method is universally accepted. Anglers can be seen like so may herons, their necks bent forward as they search the margins for fish. Often fish will give themselves away with a dorsal fin breaking the surface, but for the most part it is the sub-surface vision that is the primary sense employed by the fishermen.

It is very much the same in the USA, a country in which I have seen some extraordinary adaptations to the glasses themselves. Wearers go to huge lengths to preclude any unwanted light, with over-large peaked caps and complex side shields fitted onto the sunglass frames.

In Britain, we have ideal conditions for polaroiding, on both still and running water. Some of our smaller stillwaters are absolutely gin clear and are perfectly suited to the method. Places like Damerham or Rockbourne, where chalk spring water means that you can see the lake-bed even at depths of 12ft or more, offer superb sport, all the more so because they are now mature places with plenty of bankside cover to help in the stalking process. As a nation, we are fortunate that the vast majority of our rivers and streams are as yet free of the pollution that clouds so many continental waters, and there are innumerable trout and grayling rivers with a high degree of visibility.

It is probably worth drawing the distinction at this stage between simply using the benefits of polarising glasses in the normal course of fishing and the very different but positive act of polaroiding. The former is simply an added bonus, whereas the later is a sport in itself. It pre-supposes that the angler is setting out deliberately to enjoy this intensely visual element in his fishing, and quite often his tackle, leader rigs and flies will be geared accordingly.

I remember a glorious instance of this a few years ago, when I was fishing the Welsh Dee at Bala. It was one of those perfect fishing days, overcast but still very bright, and with little or no wind to disturb the water surface. My friend and I had to climb down a steep bank to the river and in doing so we could clearly see a large deep pool with some equally large fish shapes lurking there. As we got closer we could see that they were very large grayling, part of a larger shoal that appeared to be holding well behind the leading fish. We edged as close as we dared, still high above them on the sloping bank, and could clearly make out three exceptional fish that had taken station well ahead of the main shoal. It was a classic situation for some selective polaroiding. Having eased away from the pool, we made our way downstream so that we could approach the pool from below. A flip of a coin meant that Dennis had first crack at them, so I left my rod behind and took the camera instead. We waded together to within casting distance, and a 10yd cast took the weighted shrimp just upstream of the leading fish. Visibility was not as good from this angle as it had been from directly above, but we could still see the fly drift over the leading fish. It had been at least a foot above him, and he ignored it completely. Dennis was a fraction

Left: *A brace that fell to polaroiding tactics*

Right: *A quality 'double' from Damerham*

slow in preparing for the second cast, and before he could do anything a smaller grayling from the main shoal had surged forward to take his fly. His quick reaction in steering it downstream meant that the bigger fish remained unspooked, and after releasing the half-pounder he was ready for another throw.

We still had the three big fish clearly marked, so we edged a yard closer and dropped the second cast further upstream. This time the depth had been judged to a nicety, the big fish shifted left to intercept, and the fight was on. After quite a battle, all 2½lb of him came to net, superbly marked and in absolute prime condition. To have fished the pool 'blind' would almost certainly have produced fish, but without the visual element of the polaroiding I very much doubt that we would have seen those big fish lying well ahead of the shoal.

In its simplest form, polaroiding can be as basic as locating a fish, stalking and catching it. Yet when developed, it involves a huge amount of watercraft, precise control of fly depth, pinpoint accuracy with presentation and accurate striking. Further still, it requires careful leader construction and very close attention to the weighting of the fly patterns for that all-important depth control. It goes without saying that good eyesight is a prerequisite, but this, and all other factors, are negated without top quality polarising glasses and it would be impossible to write this article without mentioning a brand name.

Until recently, I thought that all polarising glasses were more or less the same. That was when a good friend introduced me to Serengeti. We were at Rockbourne and it must have been one of the brightest, hardest days of the year. Fish were about, but in the hot sunny conditions they were feeding well down, and for the most part they were hard to see. My fishing partner wandered up beside me and asked casually why I wasn't casting at the particular fish that was cruising past the little patch of gravel. Now eyesight is something I pride myself upon, but for the life of me I was unable to see the fish, nor could I see the gravel patch. After some fairly pointed comments about my advancing years, he offered me the use of his glasses. The revelation was as instant as it was astonishing. It was as though a switch had been thrown and the water had cleared. In fact, it was almost as though I had not been using any glasses at all, the difference was that dramatic.

From that day I have been using Serengetis and can honestly say that it has made a vast change to my fishing. Not only are they infinitely better in terms of clarity, but they are so much more comfortable to wear. The days of headaches after a long session of polaroiding are a thing of the past and I no longer suffer from the permanent frown that I used to have in high summer. The reasons for this are many and no doubt can be explained by technical terms such as spectral filters and the like, but such jargon is for opticians and not for anglers. Suffice it to say that the combination of photochromic lenses with polarising filters, combined with some of the purest clarity I have ever seen, make these the only glasses for the really serious fisherman. After Serengeti, all other glasses are just 'shades'.

Inevitably, such quality comes at a price and Serengetis offer little or no change out of £300. However, as an investment both in your angling future and your eyesight, this is not excessive. Very few items of fishing tackle will make such a difference to your catch rate as these will, and all fellow owners with whom I have spoken consider it to be money well spent. For security – I used to lose at least one pair a year in Chew – a £2 lanyard is strongly recommended.

In most instances, polaroiding does not require long casting as it is not practical to locate fish accurately at great distances. Short casting, often to fish that are less than 5yd distant, is the norm. One element of distance, however, is crucial and that is the depth of the fish in the water. This is an aspect of angling that is notoriously difficult to judge, as more often than not the fish will be deeper than you think he is. Just as in surface fishing to visibly feeding trout, your cast needs to contain some 'forward lead', to borrow an expression from the shooting fraternity. In most circumstances, and unless the fish are very high in the water, leaded flies are employed, and it is imperative that these should sink quickly and cleanly to the required depth. In the last two years, I have learned the secret from fellow anglers from Poland that such flies need to be slim and streamlined, so that they penetrate the surface with a minimum of fuss and do not contain excessive air to give unwanted buoyancy. This point is vital. All the lead weighting in the world is useless if the fly contains too much spike and bulk to retain the air, just as my old-style Hare's Ear Shrimps did. As an experiment, I have used the new slimmer flies with half the lead wire of the old patterns, and they still sink more quickly. Accurate casting is all very well, but if your fly reaches the required depth after the fish has gone past, then it is unlikely to be of much use.

Some of the best polaroiding that I have enjoyed in recent years has been at Damerham. This lovely series of small lakes has now matured to the extent where it feels totally natural, and there is abundant bankside cover for stalking and concealment. They also have their own unique strain of 'blue' trout, which are rainbows with a pronounced blue hue to their backs and flanks. They are slightly more visible in the water, but to counter this they are more easily spooked and as such they represent a real challenge.

I often feel at Damerham that the anglers who simply stick to the 'chuck and chance' methods are sadly missing out. Polaroiding in such clear water is intensely visual and can provide many hours of pleasure. It is all too easy to become absorbed and preoccupied with the sport, to the extent where time has no meaning. Hours disappear like minutes in a fascinating contest of hide-and-seek with the fish.

Although the original concept of polaroiding in Australia was primarily aimed at shallow stillwaters, probably the ultimate challenge is to be had on running water. Here we have three 'distance' elements to contend with: the length of cast, the depth of the fish in the water, and the push of the current to confound our best-laid plans. Old-fashioned and out-moded ideas about waiting for the fish to come up in the water so that dry fly can be employed, are far too restrictive. Polaroiding opens up a whole new method of fishing in such circumstances and as such it has now developed far beyond its early parameters.

Above all, I feel that it is a method of flyfishing that has yet to realise its full potential, particularly as the fly patterns are evolving so fast. In the 1991 World Flyfishing Championships I was given polaroiding flies by competitors from Poland, France and Australia. All were fundamentally different, but all had various things in common. Given the inventiveness of British fly-tyers, I think that this very special piscatorial path has many miles still to be trodden.

Winter Fishing

AS RECENTLY AS FIVE years ago I used to think that people who went flyfishing in the depths of winter were insane. I could see no attraction whatsoever in standing on some exposed bank, shivering in an icy north-easterly wind and trying to coax some unsuspecting rainbow out of their state of semi-torpor. The whole concept had no appeal and like many contemporaries I was content to hang up my rods at the end of October and wait patiently for spring.

Enlightenment and an ultimate conversion were slow in coming. In fact, it was only because of the delightful nature of the very first outing that I persevered at all, and I suspect that this is crucial to everyone's impression of winter trouting: it is all too easy to be totally disenchanted on the first trip, simply by the weather. The adage of 'once bitten, twice shy' is very relevant to winter fishing.

In the event, I agreed to try it only after a considerable amount of pressure from angling friends and colleagues. I also admit to having been a little surprised at the

Cage stocking at Ardleigh. Fish can be evenly distributed around the water, with less likelihood of shoaling

inordinate pleasure that they seemed to get from the process and there was a nagging doubt that I might have been missing out on something. After all, they were going out at least once a week without fail and one of the participants was not exactly renowned for his stoicism in poor conditions, so if he was going it couldn't be all bad.

That first day was a revelation. It was one of those gentle January days, with virtually no wind. A pale sun shone weakly from an egg-shell blue sky, but still provided an illusion of warmth through the jacket. The venue was Steeple Langford in Wiltshire and the smell of wood smoke lingered all day in the lovely Wylye valley. The setting and conditions were right, and the fish obliged with an almost suicidal abandon that meant a full quota by lunchtime. In fact, I rather think that 'lunchtime' is the key to winter fishing: it must be taken in a pub that sports good food – preferably curry or chilli – a log fire and a decent selection of real ale. The Bell at Wylye fills admirably all these prerequisites, dispensing both inner and outer warmth in excellent fashion, and it must have been an extremely rosy-cheeked band that emerged at 3pm. I was chauffeured back across-country to the Mendips in time for tea, and in one delightful day I had become totally hooked on winter trouting.

Of course, it isn't always that pleasant. By far the most important piece of advice to anyone thinking of taking up winter trouting is that you must be very selective over the weather. The 'bad' days can be very bad indeed, and it would be easy to become absolutely disillusioned in the space of less than an hour. You need to watch the weather forecast like a hawk and the vast majority of my winter days are planned after the 6 o'clock news.

. . . .

You need to be almost as selective over the venue, for there are good and bad fisheries that operate on the 'all year' principle. Those that are uncared for tend to degenerate into muddy puddles, with banks trampled to the state where they resemble a mud-slide. They offer not the slightest concession to the angler's comfort, such as tea- or coffee-making facilities, and their stocking levels leave much to be desired; it is very easy in winter to blame a lack of fish on the weather or the angler's ability, whereas in truth there are precious few fish stocked in the first place.

I also think that the very small fisheries are not best suited to winter sport. The larger lakes, with greater depth ranges and perhaps spring-fed water, offer a far better chance of good sport. More importantly, they offer genuinely sporting fish that can move freely around the lake, and may even be tempted into surface feeding on the milder days. The financial motive is often the only reason for a fishery to open its doors on a year-round basis, with the owners caring little for the quality or even the suitability of the actual fishing.

Fortunately for the angler, the choice of quality winter venues is vast and growing month by month. No longer is the facility restricted to southern-based waters as there are now winter fisheries all over Britain. Inevitably, the choice is usually governed by local availability, although it has to be said that some fisheries are worth travelling many more miles to visit, just as you would in the summer for a pilgrimage to Chew or Blagdon.

Two waters that fall easily into this category would be White Springs, at Pontardulais, near Swansea, and the aforementioned Langford Fishery in the Wylye Valley, near Salisbury. These two are different in character and setting, but still share many of the qualities that set them apart from the rest. They are larger – Langford is some 40 acres – and both have a natural spring source for their water. They have areas of considerable depth, yet at the same time they also have long shallow banks that attract fish on milder days and provide good habitat for the insect life. White Springs even has an excellent bar and restaurant overlooking the water, serving just the right sort of food to keep winter at bay.

Tactics for winter fishing vary enormously, from day to day and from venue to venue. Here again, though, there will be a surprise for some, because the popular belief is that this style of fishing is dictated by a monotonous 'chuck-and-chance' philosophy, using large and gaudy streamers. The reality is very different, and it is perfectly possible to develop a fishing style that relies on imitative or suggestive fly patterns, just as you would in the summer months. Indeed, in recent years I have spent many winter hours developing flies that have since become firm summer favourites, and these are flies that would probably never have come into being in the normal course of events.

As always, it is not so much the flies that really matter but the way in which they are fished, and herein lies the ultimate key to winter trouting. A serious reappraisal of retrieve methods is called for, along with an acute awareness of the depth at which your flies are performing. These two elements are crucial to success and lie at the very heart of things. Along with this, it follows that choice of the right line for the prevailing conditions is equally critical, and in turn this needs to be matched to a suitable leader configuration. As you can see, we are already getting a long way down the road from a basic attitude of cast-and-retrieve.

This aspect of fishing – any fishing – is what generated my interest in winter trout. It is very rewarding to think through your tactics, paying close attention to detail and to see the fruits of your labours being manifested in the form of a trout on the bank. Fish can be infuriatingly difficult at any time of the year, and when they become selective in feeding on the tiny midge hatches of January or February they can be just as challenging as they are in June or July.

If there is a key word to remember in cold weather fishing, then the word is 'slow'. Every pattern of retrieve needs to be slowed down, from the regular rhythm of pull-and-pause, through to the inching process of the snail-like figure-of-eight. In cold water fish are less inclined to expend any great energy in getting their meals and will rarely chase a fly. Unlike the long interminable follows that we get in high summer, the trout are more likely to follow only for a few yards, before turning away lethargically. The fish like to have plenty of time to make up their minds about an offering and it is all too easy to take the fly away too soon, particularly at the point of lift-off.

If we follow the logic of applying the word 'slow' to the flies themselves, then one thing becomes instantly apparent: the flies will need a good deal of in-built mobility. A fly pattern that is designed to be pulled at speed through the surface in summer needs little mobility as all the life is imparted by the retrieve. But by contrast, winter flies need to have as much natural mobility as we can give them as less life will be imparted by the actual retrieve process.

This important 'life' factor in a fly comes from various tying techniques, as well as the judicious use of certain materials. Actually, it is more a case of a combination of materials such as lead wire, marabou feathers and soft hen hackles that will link up to give the desired effect. For example, we all know and understand the uses of marabou feathers in any fly. The natural mobility of the feather fibres, responding to the tiniest movement on the leader, will give life to any fly. What is not so generally known is that the tyer can further enhance this movement by the simple expedient of tying the feather upright on the hook shank instead of in the more normal laid-back profile. This is the secret of flies like the Clifton, for example, whose vertical black marabou wing responds to the slightest touch on the fly line and gives extra life to the slowest retrieves.

The same is true of hackled flies like the Green Tag Stick Fly. Most tyers will use a red game-cock hackle at the head, and this is fine for the summer months. However, my 'winter' Stick Fly employs an ultra-soft hen hackle from a badger cape. The hen hackle has more movement, but this movement is further emphasised by the two-tone colouring of the badger feather, with its dark base and lighter tip. It is still essentially a Stick Fly, but it is designed for a very different purpose and retrieve.

In all winter fishing it is always going to be important to explore varying depths of water, so the choice of fly line is a major factor. Again, many people will hold the view that winter fishing is about fast sinkers, but this myth needs to be dispelled. It all comes back again to the slow retrieve, and slow retrieves are not easy to achieve with fast sinkers – you just end up dredging weed. The vast majority of my fishing is done with intermediate or slow-sinking lines which allow the whole process to be slowed down and to provide infinitely better fly positioning and control.

As with most rules there are exceptions, and the most notable one here is when you are using a buoyant fly like a booby. You will then need to employ the faster sinker to get the line right on the bottom, with the buoyant nymph or booby suspended above it. The most commonly made mistakes in this style of fishing is to have too long a leader, and this actually negates most of the benefits of the method. In practice, the leader can be as short as 18–20in, allowing you to fish the fly just off the lake-bed where the trout are likely to be grubbing around. The hedged-bet method here is to fish two buoyant flies are different lengths, with one at 20in and the other at around 5–6ft, to attract more active or cruising fish.

Buoyant nymphs are most emphatically not restricted to the immortal booby, and there is a lot of fun to be had from imitative or semi-imitative flies on this method. Suspender buzzers work well, and you can even tie up buoyant versions of old favourites like the pheasant tail by using polystyrene balls at the head. These can either be tied in under the dressing or as part of the pattern itself. A buoyant head with a gold rib hare's ear body is deadly, with many takes coming to the static fly. The only danger to watch out for is that you don't make the flies too buoyant, as these can restrict the sinking of the actual line and can leave you with a huge bow of sunken line and some odd-looking flies hanging in the surface. The trick is to match the amount of buoyancy to the hook wire in use; it is a simple expedient to test this in a glass of water or basin.

Fly visibility is also frequently overlooked. Very few waters qualify for the 'gin clear' description even in the summer, and winter water is often further coloured by flood water, run off or algae. If visibility drops to 2ft or less, then it will almost certainly pay to have an extra element of brightness in the fly patterns that you use. This can be as little as a fluorescent tag or butt, ranging right through to a full fluorescent wing of bright red feather or body chenille. To take the fly, the fish has first to see it - a fairly obvious equation, but one that is often surprisingly ignored.

I should perhaps confess to being a seeker of comfort in all of my fishing, and winter fishing in particular. Not for me are the windward banks, even if I am convinced that the wind will be pushing all the daphnia in that direction. I would much rather have the wind behind me, with a good jacket between me and its chilling edge. I can also drift the line around gently, without having to hurry things as always seems to be the case on the downwind banks.

Having said that, it must be pointed out that the wind is one of the most important aspects of weather for consideration, and in the choice of fishing position. Fly life is either sparse or non-existent in winter, and the staple diet of fish in waters of any size is daphnia. These little protein-rich crustaceans are completely at the mercy of wind and current, and they drift around in the water in great masses. They will shift position wherever the wind blows them, but the biggest concentrations will (almost) always be on the downwind banks, which is where the fish will look for them. Obviously they are beyond imitation at the tying bench, but daphnia-feeding fish are always on the look out for a bigger food item and they can be tempted by a whole host of patterns. Essentially, though, it is all about fish location: find the daphnia swarms and the chances are that you will also have found the fish.

British weather is nothing if not changeable and it is worth remembering that daphnia will not always be on the downwind banks. Prevailing winds for three or four days will put them there, but an overnight wind change can mean that you not only have the daphnia but also the 'comfort zone' of the wind behind you – a real bonus. It is possible to have huge concentrations of daphnia on the upwind banks, so this is yet another reason to make a careful study of the weather forecasts prior to any planned trip.

In terms of my big lake or reservoir fishing, I still subscribe to the theory that winter is for fly-tying. The fish need a break, as do the anglers, so I am happy to leave the banks to the waterfowl and other wildlife residents. But on smaller waters there is much pleasure to be had from selecting the right day. There is no finer way of working off the Christmas excesses than by taking a stroll around Langford or by seeking the ever-rising grayling of the southern streams. No doubt it will be part of the pre-season build-up again this year, but I'll still be in the pub by lunchtime!

Pot-pourri

THIS SECTION DEALS WITH a host of minor tactics, mostly concerned with methods for specific fishing conditions. During the course of my winter lectures, I can usually count on at least some of these points being raised at question time, and there seems to be much common ground in the problems and queries that anglers have. They are not listed in any particular order or given any specific degree of importance. One or two may reinforce some of the points made elsewhere in the book and I hope that the elaboration is worthwhile.

STOCK FISH

Whether you like it or not, stockies are a fact of life on virtually all stillwaters. To maintain the kind of rod averages that we have have become used to – it could be argued regrettably – fishery management are forced into what amounts to a put-and-take policy throughout the season. This, of course, takes place to a greater or lesser degree depending on the size of the water, with some of the mini ponds requiring stock on a daily basis and the big reservoirs perhaps being topped up no more than three or four times a year. Whatever the case, it is always worth monitoring your local stocking as it affects not just the stockies themselves but also the resident fish.

Stockies are much maligned creatures, wrongly so in many respects. It is true that for the first few days after stocking they can be too easy to catch, but equally I have found on many occasions that they can be infuriatingly difficult. This is especially true on the big lakes where they are reared on in lake cages, in which they will become well acclimatised to the water prior to being stocked. In any event, I prefer to treat them with a fair degree of respect and particularly for competition purposes it pays to understand a few essential facts about them.

There is absolutely no question that recently introduced stockies will 'stir up' the resident fish. On many occasions at Chew and Blagdon we have been having hard times and have welcomed the stocking wagon. In subsequent days, the resident fish – those that have hitherto appeared either absent or uncatchable – have started to fea-

Andrew Mayo strips eggs from a Blagdon Brown

Where quality begins: the rearing trays at Ubley hatchery

ture in our bags as if by magic. Furthermore, those same residents have only been caught in areas near the stockies and nowhere else. It is worth remembering, therefore, that there is no great shame in fishing the hot-spots – if you can endure the verbal slings and arrows and cries of 'stockie basher' that are bound to ensue. More seriously, it is possible to select flies in such places that the stockies are likely to ignore, which includes natural food patterns that they will be unused to seeing. Such flies can select the resident fish. Raw stockies are known to have a weakness for red and hot orange, so if you need an element of purism to make you feel better, avoid those colours.

The other worthwhile point about stockies is that they normally favour certain depths and locations after being stocked. Because of their stew-pond environment that has has been their home for so long, the walls of dams or similar features hold a certain familiarity for them. Most stews or nets/cages are no more than 10ft deep, and again the stockies like to hold at this depth, often for many weeks. If you link the two together and maybe throw in the presence of cages (where they can get a free meal), you will create the ideal stockie habitat.

For the first week after stocking, the fish also tend to come on the feed at certain times of day, as if by magic. This is almost certainly because such times are when they are used to being fed in the stews, and it is worth registering these times. Again, such sudden activity has similar effects on the residents. Stockies are gregarious and they like to hold in shoals, often for many weeks after stocking, a feature that makes it much easier to monitor changes in their behaviour.

PROBLEM DAYS

I like to think that we have covered most of the fishing conditions likely to be encountered in Britain during the course of this book, but there are one or two 'problem days' that deserve special mention, if only because they still appear to hold so many horrors for so many anglers.

The sight of a flat calm on a big reservoir used to be greeted with gloom and dismay, but largely thanks to the upsurge in use of the dries this is no longer the case – or at least it should not be. Far from being a great problem, a flat calm presents a whole range of possibilities that we are otherwise denied in any sort of ripple, and the thinking angler will welcome them. The complete range of dry-fly tactics are not only possible, but almost obligatory in a flat calm. Rise forms can be clearly seen, and by careful wading on the bank or by judicious use of the oars in the boat they can be 'stalked' and ambushed. Even a single rising fish is a challenge in a flat calm, as you can give a disproportionate amount of time to him in terms of stalking, judging forward lead and presentation.

In a similar vein, boat fishing in a flat calm with sinking lines becomes a matter of the utmost precision. With the boat being near static, there is much more sensitivity and feel as to what is taking place at the business end. You have infinitely more control than, say, in a big wave when everything happens so fast. When becalmed you can explore the varying depths more effectively, perhaps using a half-hour each on intermediate, sinker and then fast sinker. Within this, varying count-down times can be employed, allowing all water levels to be fully investigated. You can also fish much deeper with sinking lines than would normally be the case, using a kind of extended 'hold-and-draw' with up to 20yd of fly line.

It goes without saying that watercraft is at a premium in a flat calm, as any noise or disturbance is magnified tenfold. Make full use of all the natural features: in boat fishing, look for any shade from bankside trees or use the natural barrier of a weed-bed. I have even nudged the boat up against semi-submerged tree stumps on Chew, both for further stability and camouflage.

The other problem day that seems to cause worry is when it is a near gale. With wind and wave making life decidedly uncomfortable, many anglers will give in and head for the pub. Unfortunately, competition dates do not take the weather into account and you may have no option but to fish. The crucial factor here is control, or rather the lack of it. Bank anglers can almost always find either a lee bank or at least a favourable angle, but boats are at the full mercy of the elements. Everything happens so fast that it is virtually impossible to retain any level of subtlety at all, and my own yardstick here is simply to stick to basics: forget that yesterday's practice seemed to dictate slow sinker and nymphs and change to line and flies that you can control. This may be floating line and big palmers or bumbles, or it may be a fast sinker with attractors. The problem with the latter is that even with a good drogue you will still be forced to retrieve fairly soon after the cast, otherwise too big a bow develops in the line. This means that you will have to forget fishing the flies any deeper than around the 10ft mark, unless a sheltered bank can be found.

The plus factor in a gale is that all the food items tend to get nicely disturbed and tumbled into varying levels of water, and this in turn encourages the fish to feed more generally and with greater abandon. Trout seem to enjoy playing in the waves, hitting into a bushy Soldier with some gusto, and these conditions often provide very positive takes. Personally, I like to try to position the boat downwind of an underwater feature such as a big weed-bed or false island, where fish are likely to be found taking the food items that get washed down.

Purely for safety and comfort, I often reduce the casting length in a big wind, perhaps down to 20yd or less. Short lining in a gale is an art form developed to a nicety by the Irish who relish such conditions, and it can apply to both sinking and floating lines. It is also somewhat more friendly to your boat partner, as it is nearly impossible to avoid dropping the line at some stage during the day because of the prolonged effort involved.

'ILLUMINATED' AREAS

This is a minor boat-fishing tactic, but a relevant one. In certain conditions of light, most notably early morning and late afternoon, the angle of the sun can combine with the ripple to give good visibility on one side of the boat and near-impossible conditions on the other. We have all seen it, that kind of magnesium colour that merges water and sky together to the extent where even the most obvious rise cannot be seen. These 'illuminated' areas can last for hours and the sporting thing to do is to share the good end of the boat with your partner. Even the very best sunglasses are no match for these conditions and in some competitions I have changed ends as fre-quently as every half hour, just to keep things fair.

NETTING

This applies more to boat than to bank fishing, although the rule is just the same: in competitions, never let anyone net your fish. Apart from the friction that a clumsy netting or lost fish can involve, there is no way that anyone else, including the best gillies in the world, will be able to do the job better than yourself. The reason is that only the angler can gauge the exact moment to put the net in the water and only the angler can co-ordinate the two movements of net and rod to do the job properly. This is one of the few things in fishing that is clearly definable and totally beyond question.

BOAT PARTNERS

Boat partners need to be chosen with great care. Empathy with a regular boat part-ner is bound to accrue in time, and it is obviously preferable to share days afloat with someone who at least enjoys the same style of fishing, if not a matching philosophy. Fishermen on the whole are very nice people, but I tend to avoid pipe smokers, who have an uncanny habit of tapping out pipes on the thwarts, incessant talkers, who chatter all day about nothing, calling for automatic replies such as 'yes' or 'really?' or 'hmmm' and people who forget to bring a bottle of wine which makes a good natural break in the day and allows time for thoughts to be collected and tactics reviewed.

FIRST CHOICE

On any day's boat fishing, there can be a problem over choosing the first drifts. In the absence of visible fly life, stockies shoals or any surface movement, my own rule-of-thumb is to head for the shallows. Water that is about 10ft deep is by far the best place to be if any kind of doubt exists. The exceptions to this are what I would term unnatural features – aerators, for instance – that can normally be relied upon for a better-than-average chance of a fish.

COMPETITION ATTITUDE

While I try to make my competitive days as near as possible to a normal day's fishing, I am bound to say that there is sometimes an element of adrenalin involved. Competition days are about thought and concentration, with a full mental checklist of tackle to be prepared, flies to be sorted and provisional plans to be made. A little adrenalin is a good thing as it sharpens the senses, but too much of it is counter-productive, as one or two notorious members of the shaky hand/chain-smoking brigade will testify.

Boat partners from many nations compete at top international level. Sign language provides communication, and shared information is vital

Strange things can happen! Even the roach like nymphs at Chew, and their fry are important food items

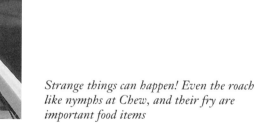

'Horsing' a fish to the net at Dreux, France (European Cup)

SUSPENDER BUZZERS

I purposely avoided the inclusion of suspender buzzers in the dry-fly section because they are so unlike any other dry pattern. Whereas the majority of dries are fished on or in the surface film, suspenders are actually fished (in most cases) beneath the film, a factor that is crucial to their success.

As a fly pattern, the suspender could not be easier to tie. A light wire gauge hook is required and a slim seal's fur body is tied from just around the bend to just behind the eye, ribbed with fine wire for durability. A ball of Ethafoam or polystyrene is then tied at the head, large enough to keep the fly hanging tail-down beneath the surface film. Too much buoyancy will mean that the fly floats unnaturally and too little will make it sink. Experimentation is needed to find the right amount of buoyancy for the particular hook you are using. Body colours of seal's fur (or substitute) can be varied, but the best size for these patterns is unquestionably a standard shank 12.

Suspenders are best fished static and in much the same way as you would an emerger. They can have their day and although I still prefer to fish more conventional dries, there are occasions, especially when the fish are taking non-emerging pupae below the surface, when they are obligatory. I should stress, though, that they are, for me at any rate, a minor tactic within the overall dry-fly method.

A suspender can also perform a fundamentally different role as a 'dropper' when booby fishing. On cold days in winter, or as a part of your best-bet prospecting system under the percentage method, a suspender fished with a booby can work. Leader length will depend on other factors, such as whether you are boat or bank fishing, depth of water or density of weed-beds. However, as a general rule you will fish the suspender at around 2ft from the fly line, with the booby at about 5–6ft. It makes an interesting variation on the theme.

SCALE DOWN

One of the most frequent questions that I am asked at my winter lectures concerns the use of very small flies. One look at the fly section later in the book will show that favoured sizes are almost universally in the 10 to 14 range, but there are occasions when these are too big.

Small flies on stillwater are the 16s and 18s and their use is almost always in 'fussy fish' situations. Many of our flies exaggerate not only the shape and profile but also the size of natural food items, to the extent that most of us over-estimate the size of the actual insects. When fish are being selective it pays to be aware of this factor and to offer them a closer copy in terms of size. By definition and because small flies lose all their life if they are tied on large diameter nylon, it also means fishing a finer leader to ensure compatibility between the fly and leader. As a useful yardstick, I would normally fish size 16s and 18s on 3lb super-strength nylon, and this is particularly important with the dries.

BOW WAVERS

Bow-waving fish – those that follow interminably and then turn away at the last moment – are notoriously hard to catch. Floating-line dibbling may help, but there are other minor tactics that can be employed.

Speeding up the retrieve and then stopping dead can work, as can FTA variations in an otherwise steady retrieve rate. I also like to take the flies away from the fish with a sudden lift-off and then re-present them all in one movement, which seems to help them make up their minds. If angles are available, I also would try lifting off and re-presenting at an oblique angle, with extra forward lead. It can be wrong in these circumstances to bring the flies right back to the boat, as a fish that is nervous or uncommitted is unlikely to take once he feels the boat's presence. Lifting the flies up to dibble at a 10yd range is more profitable.

GOOD THINGS

There is a resistance among anglers to give the fish too much of a good thing. By this I mean that if there are hundreds of red midge hatching and the spooning shows that the fish are really on them, there is a strong case to offer the fish three identical flies on a cast. Despite this, you will often hear anglers declaring that they like a varied
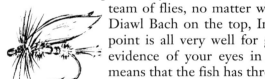
team of flies, no matter what. A cast that is 'nicely balanced' with a Diawl Bach on the top, Invicta in the middle, and Stick Fly on the point is all very well for general prospecting, but it is denying the evidence of your eyes in a red midge hatch. Three identical flies means that the fish has three chances of seeing the right fly.

WAKE FLIES

Wake flies – those patterns that rely on surface disturbance for their true effect – are flies that can be improved with a little exaggeration. Mini-muddlers, bushy palmers and particularly the bumbles can be tied with excess materials for those big wave days. In all the confusion of tumbling water and foam, the fly needs to stand out to be recognised, and I like to have at least a few of them in a box for such conditions. A size 10 Soldier with up to four palmered hackles might look awful when dry, but when pulled fast in a gale it has much to commend it.

DIBBLING

The lovely art of dibbling pulled flies is at the very heart of loch-style fishing yet true exponents are rare. This is because many people think they are dibbling, whereas in reality they are only holding the flies for a few seconds before lift-off. Proper dibbling involves lifting the rod while there are still many yards left to retrieve, and working them up to the boat. By laying the rod from side to side you can change direction on the dibble, and it is also good tactics to let the flies fall back a little and then relift, if conditions permit. I have seen Irish anglers who hold the flies on the dibble for up to a full minute, sound in the belief that there is an undecided fish beneath them. Such confidence is often well placed.

INDUCED TAKE

Fishing the induced take on running water is an accepted fact of life and is a major tactic. Why then should it not be so on stillwater? The answer is that relatively few people are prepared to try it, and of course the less exposure that a method is given the less it will be practised.

In some ways the induced take can form part of the FTA retrieve, but this is only part of the story. On small stillwaters, and as part of the polaroiding technique, it is most viable; when fish are patrolling near the bank it is easy to drop the fly to the bottom, and then to lift it in front of a cruising trout. This can also be done 'blind' on the bigger lakes; after all, the whole method of 'on the hang' involves the use of induced take. The key is to have an inherent belief that a fish is looking at your fly almost all the time, something that is probably far more true than we realise. This adds a great deal of meaning to our otherwise monotonous pull-and-pause retrieves and can become a very specific tactic for fishing over known ditches or holes.

BRAIDED LOOPS

One of the latest developments in tackle is the loop-to-loop system of braided leader. This is much more than a development on a theme, as although we have have had loop systems for some years, none have been as good as these and none have offered the same level of flexibility.

The system is marketed by Airflo and covers every possible combination from high floating to ultra-fast sink sections. Moreover, they can be combined or interchanged; for example, in New Zealand in 1991 I used a fast-sink leader section matched to an intermediate line for probing between weed-beds and a super-fast leader on a floater as a perfect substitute for a sink-tip fly line. Such leaders are now perfectly acceptable under most competition rules and their full potential is yet to be explored.

PLAYING

There are almost infinitely variable ways of playing fish and everyone has their own preference. Some like to exert hardly any pressure at all, allowing the fish to take as much time and line as he likes, while others prefer to be hard on them, almost horsing them to the net as quickly as possible. Playing a fish is either one of the sport's great pleasures or merely a means to an end – it depends on the individual attitude of mind.

. . . .

Left: *Control in the stern. A big fish takes Martin Cottis right round the boat*

Right: *Use all the angles to play the fish from a boat, but if possible keep him on the front of the boat. A fish that gets behind you, especially in a big wave, will be hard to get back*

For me, it is the point of contact with the fish that provides the greatest pleasure – the actual process of deception. Once that moment is passed and he is hooked I tend to be harder on him than most, preferring to bring him to the net as quickly as possible. Apart from the fact that he is less likely to work the hook loose, there is the very real benefit that he is less likely to become exhausted after a short fight, and this is significant as nowadays I tend to release most of my fish.

Playing a fish hard and fast is an added bonus in competitions, where time is of the essence. The competition angler who takes an age to play each fish is certainly not being fair to his boat partner, and anyone who lets the fish go around the boat half a-dozen-times is hardly playing the game. Where possible, I also like to net the fish at the back of the boat, well away from my boat partner who can continue to fish the drift. To summarise, I think that far fewer fish are lost through playing them firmly than would be the case in reverse.

In 95 per cent of instances, I prefer to play fish by hand rather than on the reel. Primarily this is because there is better control on the hand and you can feel every turn the fish makes, but also because it is possible to react much more quickly when the fish comes towards you. More fish are lost through giving slack than for any other reason.

. . . .

PART 4

COMPETITIONS

W hen I first planned the outline of this book, the intention was to resist a large chapter or section on competition fishing. This was not meant in any way to under-value the subject matter, for as many will know I am a devoted advocate of the value of competitions to the sport in general, but rather because I see the whole book as being relevant to competition methods and tactics. The way that I fish on a 'normal' day is little different from that in competitions, and the adoption of a style that is based on small and (mostly) imitative flies comes within most competition rules. It could be argued that there is in fact no need for this chapter, or indeed to make any separate distinctions.

On reflection, however, there are some points to be made. The very principle of competitive flyfishing comes in for a degree of criticism, much of which is either misguided, ill-informed, or simply just prejudiced, so there is a need for supporters of competitions to stand up and be counted. It is a fascinating branch of the sport, immensely pleasurable, and at the top levels can require every bit as much commitment as do the more 'identifiable' sports that are played with a ball or racquet.

Despite the rantings of the anti-competition brigade – and these are a relatively small number as is often the case with my 'anti' group – competitive flyfishing is hugely popular. What is more, that popularity is still growing, as ever more anglers discover the pleasures to be had form the sport. Competitions seek only to promote what is good in the sport, and most rules restrict participants to the traditional and ethical ways of fishing that have been established over many generations. In the face of some of the behaviour witnessed by non-competitive anglers these days, it is no bad thing that there are still formal bodies to promote these aspects.

The level of ability at the top of the sport is high. To be consistently successful demands commitment, as well as progressive thinking. In the past years it has largely been competition anglers who have pioneered innovation, with key individuals discovering new families fly patterns, new concepts on approach and revised techniques. Within the ranks of competition anglers you will find those who have come up with

The 'rolling start

*European Grand Slam
winners (team event) 1990*

*One of the writer's crowning
moments: individual
European Champion*

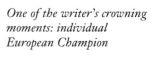

flies such as the Shipman's Buzzers, those who have developed and promoted the light line philosophy, and others who have invented nuances of technique such as hold-and-draw. In the main, such anglers are held in high regard by most observers as they consistently demonstrate that the luck factor can be reduced to a very low level. Given the many thousands that enter world or national eliminators every year, it is significant that the same names have been able to win outright on more than one occasion. The reasons are not hard to see. All sports progress through a healthy element of competition, and angling is no exception. Tackle developments, the refining of new tactics and techniques, all move forward because of those innovative fishermen who are prepared to pioneer new methods, In coarse fishing it is just the same, and it is due to the generosity of the top few in the game who are prepared to share their theories with the rest that the overall body of anglers moves ahead.

Not surprisingly, the achievements of these top men are envied by many and everyone seeks to emulate them. One of the easiest ways of getting close to the high-profile competition fishers is simply to join them. In the Benson & Hedges championship, for instance, you never know how the draw for boat partners will turn out: on one day you may have somebody new to competitions like yourself, yet on another you may be lucky enough to get drawn with John Pawson or Jeremy Lucas, or one of the many big names. A day like this is a real opportunity and an alert angler cannot fail to learn something from such an experience.

Most of the major events have their roots firmly bedded at club level. To qualify for England in the Home International series you must first register with your local federation. Regional eliminators follow, culminating in the national final, when up to a hundred anglers compete for the coveted places in the national squad for the following year. Club level is also where the Benson & Hedges tournament starts, an annual event that has done more than any other to promote competitions as a whole.

Competitive flyfishing always has a certain edge to it at whatever level, but never more so than when teamwork is involved. The ever-present fear of letting down your fellow anglers acts as a spur in itself, but even worse than that is the fear that a poor performance might affect next season's team selection.

From a team captain's point of view, the pressures are magnified tenfold. If a team is successful, then he shares in their reflected glory. But if it fails, the long finger of accusation is pointed unerringly in his direction; the scapegoat mentality is alive and well, and as much a part of flyfishing as it is in cricket or football. So, the formation and running of a successful team is about a lot more than plain good luck. It involves a whole range of things from organisational work to man management – and on occasions, a very broad pair of shoulders.

The step from club level to full international competition is inevitably a big one, with a new set of challenges. Teamwork is still vital both in the home series and the World Flyfishing Championships, but there is an element of individual performance needed to get through all the elimination stages. The numbers run into thousands in the elimination process towards the coveted twenty places for the England Home International squad, and to be even considered for the world team you have to have fished in the Home International squad as a prerequisite. Other Home International Nations have similar systems, ensuring that only those anglers who

Lunchtime vino is near compulsory; a time to relax and reflect

are prepared to make the commitment and who can demonstrate a high consistency of performance will represent their country. To win regularly at this level has little to do with luck.

Competitive flyfishing has outgrown the confines of the British Isles, and is now a truly international affair. The European Cup is a three-leg event, held in France in the spring, in England during the summer, and in Belgium in the autumn. The World Championships currently attract upwards of twenty nations each year from as far afield as Scandinavia, the USA, Canada, Australia and New Zealand, as well as the majority of Eastern and Western European countries. The popularity of the sport is visibly increasing and looks certain to continue to do so. The social side of the event is tremendous, with a wonderful exchange of views, tactics and flies between anglers of fundamentally different persuasions and cultures. It would be a very insensitive competitor who did not learn something by sharing a day with a Czech fishing rolled nymph on the rivers or from watching the French at work with their tiny dry flies.

All the tactics outlined in this book are relevant to competition fishing on stillwater and many can easily be adapted to running water. On stillwater, the only competition rule that is at odds with some of the methods described is the one concerning leaded or weighted flies, which are banned under the Home International rules. Hook technology has already come to our aid in this respect, as there are now some very heavy wire hook patterns that can compensate for the absence of lead weight. On a wider scale, barbless hooks are gaining popularity in those competitions that are fished to a catch-and-release rule, and when such hooks are properly designed they show only the slightest difference in hook-hold capabilities than their barbed counterparts.

Many people see catch-and-release as the way forward in the future, and certainly it helps to refute some of the strident arguments of the anti-competition brigade. It is already the norm in both European and World Championships, and it cannot be too long before it is universally adopted. It may also have the additional benefit of lowering the overall cost of fishing in Britain, which is only held at such high levels by virtue of the cost of stocked fish to the fishery owners. Many feel that a brace of fish for a day's sport is ample, with an option to continue to fish catch-and-release. It may be a year or so away, but it is coming.

Anxious faces at the weigh-in

So for me competition fishing is no different from any other days on the water, certainly in terms of tactics and technique. It actually increases my overall fishing time, because I would never dream of fishing a major match without first having a practice day; these days, taken to try to unlock some of the secrets of the water in question in terms of the productive locations, preferred flies and fish-holding areas, are undertaken as much for a confidence boost as anything else, as well as to focus the concentration and commitment. Companionship is also important on practice sessions, and two anglers fishing a boat or bank together will be better placed to explore a range of tactics. With both of them fishing different line densities and different fly patterns, a picture of the water will build up remarkably quickly.

I suppose the only factor that changes on competition day is the level of concentration that is applied. Normal days are slightly more relaxed, with perhaps a bottle of wine at lunchtime, whereas top-level competition requires absolute attention at all times. Good eyesight is a must, and the angler who can spot fish at maximum range and can cover those fish with accuracy and a minimum of false casting will win the day. Much is talked about the 'X' factor of the top-competition anglers or the extra feel and touch that they have. For me, this is not nearly as mystical as it might sound, as with experience and commitment this feel will come. It must be nurtured and developed; it cannot be taught or bought, but with time it can be attained.

One of the great truths in flyfishing is that we take great delight in making things more difficult for ourselves. We are forever using finer nylon, small flies and trying to deceive the most impossible fish from the impossible lie. If it were all too easy we wouldn't do it, and it is surely the challenge that brings us back again and again to the water. Arguably, the greatest challenge of all can be found in competitions, pitting your abilities not just against the fish and the weather, but against other anglers who are all looking for better methods and technique than yourself. In such situations, the sport cannot help but make progress.

. . . .

An immaculate residential Rainbow from Chew

PART 5

FLY-TYING

F ew people would argue that fly-tying is an integral part of our sport or even that it is obligatory if one is to become better than an 'average' fly fisher. The barest level of competence in tying will almost always give an edge over the inevitable restrictions of shop-bought flies, which are necessarily mass-produced and tied to rigid specifications. This implies no criticism whatsoever to such flies, as the current levels of quality are very high. Rather it is that shop-bought patterns are unlikely either to match local insect or food items correctly or to be available in the right colour or size ranges. At best they are adequate, but at worse they will fall to pieces after five minutes in the water.

There is a huge amount of pleasure to be had from tying your own flies. The actual process of creation, when a bare hook is transformed into a thing of some beauty by the addition of fur or feather, is greatly rewarding. In the winter months fly-tying can be a therapy in itself, a meaningful and productive substitute for fishing. The sense of achievement in catching a fish on a fly of your own creation is very real, and the successful completion of a complex pattern in the vice is a joy that never pales.

For most of us, it is enough simply to be able to tie flies that catch fish. My own efforts are humble in the extreme – suitably scathing comments have been passed on them in the past – and I make no claims to greatness. It is enough for me that the fish do not seem to be able to tell the difference between a whip-finish and a half-hitch, and that enough of them seem to grab hold during the course of most seasons. It pays to be aware of one's limitations in life and I am fully aware that my fly-tying prowess would not qualify me for any mentions in despatches.

There are, however, a growing number of people for whom fly-tying is little short of an obsession. They are able to elevate it from simply being a necessary part of the sport into an art form, reaching effects of realism and levels of proficiency that are way beyond we lesser mortals. When they open their fly-boxes you get the distinct feeling that some of the contents are going to crawl out and bite you, so lifelike are the creations. They are, without question, true artists in their own field and are fully deserving of our admiration.

Such growing enthusiasm is due in no small way to the interest generated by the Benson & Hedges fly-tying competition, which is in many cases a celebration of the art as much as a competition. With classes for beginners, intermediates and masters, it attracts huge entries and has been responsible for the pioneering of new tying techniques as well as inventive new uses for established materials. The standard of entries seems to get progressively higher each season, and the competition attracts tyers from all over Britain as well as Europe.

No sport develops by standing still and without any question fly-tying is an evolutionary art. The number and quality of tying materials available is amazing, not to say bewildering, and is a far cry from the simple pieces of fur and feather used by past generations. The fact that the past masters had such basic tools and materials to work with speaks volumes for their ability, and modern generations owe them a great debt for the legacy of such immortal patterns as the Mallard and Claret, Dunkeld, and the like.

With all the tools and gadgets currently available, and with the plethora of materials from every corner of the world, it is hardly surprising that beautiful flies are being produced. However, it is not just the materials but also the techniques being used that makes these modern creations so good. In some areas – seal's fur, for example – synthetic materials have replaced natural fibres with a revision or rethinking needed as to how they should be applied. Anyone who has compared the use of Antron on the one hand with seal's fur or hare's ear on the other will understand that there is some considerable difference in the simple term 'dubbing'.

But of all the great forward strides in recent years surely the most significant must be in the field of hooks. Of all the items of tackle that we buy, hooks are probably the cheapest, yet they are arguably the most important. This is an area in which no financial short-cuts should be taken – there is absolutely no substitute for quality.

HOOKS FOR EVERY PURPOSE

It is a fact of life that the quality of the flies that we tie and use is directly related to the quality of the hooks upon which we tie them. The finest tying in the world is completely negated if the hook barb is cut too deeply or if the tempering has not been completed, or even if the combination of eye, shank and bend has been badly engineered.

Readers will know by now that I am very much in favour of the principle of matching the hook to the fly. For too many years, tyers just picked up the first hook that they came to in the kit and tied on it. Little thought was given to the shape of the hook, its wire gauge or anything to do with its suitability for the fly pattern being tied. Now tyers are becoming increasingly aware of the importance of wire gauge and the effects that this can have on the way the fly looks and performs in the water. The simple message of fine wires for dries and emergers, medium wires for wet flies and nymphs, and heavy-gauge wires for deep nymphs has been preached by myself and many others, and a degree of enlightenment exists.

Even so, it can be difficult and even the experts are likely to be baffled by the vast array of hook patterns on the market. The most important first lesson is to avoid the 'cheap and nasty' hooks. You are going to spend ten minutes or more of your life

Hook inspection at Partridge of Redditch; good products from an all-British company

Below left: *This shadow-graph picture shows all the key points of a well-engineered hook*

Below right: *Good quality hooks: a strong, keen point is matched to a small but effective barb. The round bend format offers good hook-hold, with plenty of gape*

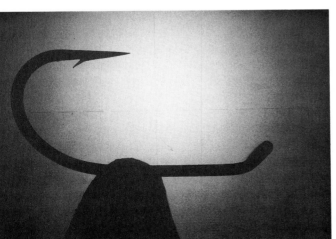

tying the fly, and to do this on a poor quality hook makes no sense at all. Even the best hooks are not expensive when viewed against the overall cost of fishing. Always buy the best you can afford from one of the famous and reputable names.

Hook technology has changed dramatically in the last decade, primarily with the advent of what is termed 'chemical sharpening'. This is a system that permits very fine points to be produced that are incredibly strong and durable. Contrary to popular belief, this process is not solely restricted to imports from the Far East, as British manufacturers now use a directly comparable process. Most notable among these manufacturers is the traditional English firm of Partridge of Redditch, who produce a series of hooks called 'Grey Shadow'. These are 'flashpointed', which is another word for chemical sharpening, and they also have a superb Niflor finish which makes them very durable. Rusty points and barbs are a thing of the past, and in this respect they are far superior to their Japanese counterparts.

So what constitutes a balanced hook selection in the tying kit? Do we really need all the endless variations that we read about, with all the weird shapes and designs? The answer is an emphatic 'no', as it is perfectly feasible to restrict yourself to three hook patterns for all your tying and this will cover all eventualities. It is true that some specialist hooks are worth considering, particularly if you intend to tie flies for competitions or if you want to get that extra degree of realism into the finished fly.

You will only need hooks for dries, wet fly and nymph. However, it helps to have variety in hook-shank length, and a longer nymph hook is also a 'double-purpose' hook as it can also be used for lures. I have drawn up the following shortlist of eight hook styles that will provide you with every conceivable fly you will ever need to tie:

1 Captain Hamilton wet fly (Partridge GRS2A). A brilliant all-rounder for wet flies, smaller nymphs and buzzers.
2 Kamasan B160 grub hook. A wide gape hook, particularly useful in the smaller sizes. Perfect for shrimp patterns and buzzers.
3 Kamasan B170. A lighter wire hook for traditionals and for dry fly and emergers.
4 Partridge H1A. One of my all-time favourites. A classic longer-shank nymph hook. Ideal for Stick Fly, Montana, Pheasant Tail, etc. Good medium wire gauge.
5 Kamasan B175. A heavier wire wet fly and nymph hook. Very strong and heavier to get flies down in the water.
6 Partridge Stronghold nymph hook. One of the strongest and heaviest wire nymph hooks on the market. It is great for Damsels, Pheasant Tails and also for some of the mini-attractor patterns that demand a heavy hook.
7 Partridge 'Living Nymph' hook. One of the best new hooks for many years, this one has almost limitless possibilities. The shape and wire gauge are just right and the finished flies look incredibly lifelike.

Top right: *Ideal emerger conditions*
Below far right: *Maximum sidestrain to keep the fish from the weeds*
Below right: *A classic brownie from Rutland's South Arm*

8 Partridge 'Detached Body' nymph hook. Rather more for the specialist tyers, this one is for the ultra-realistic nymphs such as Damsels. A near perfect body shape can be achieved.

If I had to restrict the above list even further I would be happy to use only numbers 1, 4, 5 and 6 – these will cover upwards of 90 per cent of my tying.

DEEP FLIES FOR DOUR DAYS

What about those dour, miserable days of summer, when no fish are showing any-where and the lake looks lifeless, making any sort of surface fishing absolutely use-less? Well, you shouldn't just admit defeat and head for the pub; in reality there are many things you can do, one of which is to go prospecting with some deep nymphs.

How many times have you caught fish and spooned them in the summer? On an apparently lifeless water the deep nymph can produce good fish, and the use of a marrow spoon to examine the stomach contents will often reveal that they have, in fact, been feeding very strongly. The fact that we can't actually see such feeding because it occurs deep in the lake is of no importance. They are still feeding and that's what counts. Once fish get into a good summer feeding pattern it takes more than dour weather to stop them, and they will invariably be foraging, at least to some degree, throughout the day. The trick is to know what they are likely to be looking for and to gear your fly selection accordingly.

Food items for deep-feeding fish are most likely to fall into three categories. On occasions they may be looking for corixa, snails or other bugs, but mostly the ones that matter are midge pupae, sedge pupae and damsels. The general imitations for these insects are well known, as are the general suggestive patterns of Pheasant Tail, Stick Fly, and suchlike. The problem sometimes occurs when tyers don't give enough thought to how they apply the lead weight, that all-important ingredient in any weight pattern. Badly applied weight can not only spoil the look of the fly and the way in which it fishes, but it can actually impair the hooking qualities as well, which is a major problem. The diagrams below illustrate this clearly:

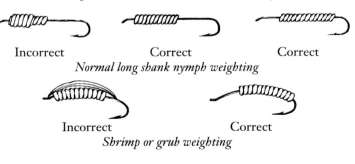

| Incorrect | Correct | Correct |

Normal long shank nymph weighting

| Incorrect | Correct |

Shrimp or grub weighting

Top left: *Aerial shot of Blagdon at high water. The ultimate assessment of contour, with weed-beds and the deep water fall-off clearly visible*

Below left: *The epitome of Loch Style*

Apart from applying too much lead wire, which is the most common problem, most anglers don't give enough thought about the actual lead that they use. I have even seen magazine articles that recommend the use of wine-bottle lead foils, which might be economical, but most definitely is not practical. The use of a lead wire that is too thick is just as much of a problem and you should always use fine gauge wire – apart from the really huge hook sizes (8 or above).

By using finer wire you can build up the right amount of weight for each specific pattern and also the correct shape for the finished fly. For all my trying I use the 0.37mm gauge wire from Veniard, which I find ideal.

Shaped bodies, for example leaded shrimps, can be formed by laying multiple layers of wire on top of the hook shank rather than continually winding them around the shank. The latter will build up too much bulk in the hook gape, resulting in a poor hook-hold and many missed takes. The same applies to the smaller weighted nymphs like Damsels and Pheasant Tails, where too heavy a wire near the hook gape can have disastrous effects.

You may also have problems if you use too much wire or too heavy a wire gauge, as these can form a body that is altogether too bulky. The vast majority of underwater nymphs are slim, even streamlined, and flies like damsels taper finely near the tail. It therefore follows that we should concentrate the lead wire at the head and thorax of any pattern rather than at the tail for both of these very good reasons.

One further benefit of this is that most flies will swim more attractively when weighted in this way, especially if a little marabou or other mobile feather is employed at the tail. Front-weighting will give the fly an enticing up-and-down movement, very similar to the swimming motion of most aquatic nymphs.

FLY-TYING – THE FUTURE

I firmly believe that the modern approach to competitive flyfishing has played its part in the development of the fly-tying art. In an age when international barriers both seen and unseen are being torn down, there is an increasing dialogue between anglers of all nations. Angling has a culture that is common to all countries, yet it is fascinating to see the different interpretations that are placed on common problems. For instance, the majority of English nymph patterns rely primarily on a dubbed body, whereas one look at a continental fly-box, and certainly one belonging to a Pole or a Czech angler, will reveal flies that are almost always woven.

The rediscovery (for it is certainly not a new technique) of woven flies came as a revelation to the England flyfishing squad. We were amazed to see that woven flies had almost twice the sink rate of dubbed nymphs of exactly the same weight, as their super-slim profile cut cleanly through the water. Moreover, with no trapped air pockets, which are an inevitable fact of life with dubbed bodies, they were far less buoyant. In events such as the World Championships, where anglers from twenty or more nations meet, compete and communicate, there is an exchange of views that can only be to the good of our sport. The fact that fly patterns are also exchanged is a bonus.

Modern synthetics feature prominently in many of the flies that I use and as well as replacing some traditional materials they have also opened up new techniques in

Variation on a theme: this shows just how many ways there are to interpret a standard pattern, in this case the Elk Hair Sedge

tying. These are numerous, ranging from the use of pearl tinsel underbodies over-wrapped with clear ribbings, through to the melted nylon 'eyes' of a damsel, or the rubber legs of a girdle bug, or the spectraflash wing-case of a hare's ear. Barely a generation ago, it was unlikely that anyone would have thought of using chain bead eyes on a lure, or Latex dental dam for a caddis, or polystyrene balls for a booby, yet nowadays all are commonplace. It follows, therefore, that there will be more such revelations around the corner, waiting to be discovered by some forward-thinking tyer who is toying with some experimental patterns on some quiet evening at the bench. All it needs is the spark of an idea for the next Dunkeld/Stick Fly/Hopper classic to evolve.

It is a sobering thought that some of the doyens of angling were able to create the masterpieces of their generation with only the barest rudiments of tools and materials. The up-winged marvels of the halcyon chalkstream days are truly remarkable, and the olives or nymphs of Halford and Skues were in those times considered to be revolutionary. The scene has been flavoured by international offerings from Wulff and Schweibert, as well being given a contentious note by Walker or Housby. Present-day masters are more numerous and the immaculate tyings of Terry Griffiths, Oliver Edwards, Charles Jardine and Peter Gathercole, among others, cannot fail to impress. Creations from their vices are works of art, within the state of the art, and we lesser mortals can only sit in open-mouthed admiration.

Fly-tying is like music or wine. Just as there will always be another melody and another vintage, so too will there always be new flies. There will be new boundaries of realism to be crossed, just as there will also be some fundamentally simple fish-catching patterns. As in the past, they will come from the vices of master and pupil alike. Fishing is one of the few pleasures in life that makes no discrimination.

PART 6

THE FLIES

For any angling writer, the selection of any shortlist of flies is fraught with danger. There will always be some hawk-eyed reader who will point out an obvious omission, and equally there will always be the sceptic who insists that you are keeping some 'specials' up your sleeve. It is a classic 'no win' scenario for the author.

It is worth making the point again, therefore, that it is not so much the fly that matters but how it is fished. In general terms it is the life and movement that the angler imparts to the fly that catches the fish, coupled essentially with the way in which it is presented. The best flies in the world are of no use at all if they are badly fished, yet at the same time the scruffiest creations can always score in the hands of an expert.

Almost all of this book is about the flies and the ways in which they should be fished. Even so, the work would not be complete without some sort of shortlist, or without a brief description of the history and tying detail of each pattern. The list is by no means exhaustive and I have to admit to being a hoarder of flies; I have far too many boxes full of weird and wonderful creations that at best are one-offs, and for the most part will probably never be used. They have been collected on a myriad of fishing trips and are tangible proof that many flies are designed to catch fishermen and not fish.

Even so, the 'serious' fly-boxes, for want of a better term, are all full of the flies featured on the following pages. There is a much used quotation that says that about 80 per cent of the fish are caught on less than dozen fly patterns, and this is not wide of the mark. It is true that successful flies tend to get used by more people, more often, and because of this they naturally catch more fish. Care must therefore be taken that we do not get blinkered by the famous flies and that we are prepared to experiment with new patterns from time to time. Even so, it is undeniable that a shortlist of outstanding patterns does exist, and it would be a foolish angler who ignored them.

As far as possible I have categorised each fly, although it will quickly become apparent that some patterns can and do defy any labels. Some will bridge the supposed gap between imitative and suggestive, while others have multiple roles to play in that they are both suggestive and close-copy, depending on how they are fished. In fact, it is the supreme versatility of most of these flies that marks them out as being special and draws us back to them time after time, year after year. For ease of reference, the flies are divided into four principal categories.

Hawthorn

Traditional Wet Flies

THIS GROUP OF PATTERNS contains some of the true household names in flyfishing. Potentially, the list is endless, but I have restricted it here to just a famous few, as these are flies that no serious angler can afford to be without.

Sedge pupa

CONNEMARA BLACK

There are so many aspects of game fishing that have their origins in history, and particularly in the history of Scotland and Ireland. Lock style fishing was developed many generations ago on the loughs and lakes of those lovely countries, and the Irish were fishing from free-drifting boats long before our earliest stillwaters were a twinkle in the developer's eye.

It is hardly surprising, therefore, that many of the best fly patterns in use today have their backgrounds in these places. Flies like the Dunkeld, the Peter Ross and the Connemara Black are eternal patterns. They have stood the test of time, which is the hardest taskmaster of all, and they are as good today as when they were first invented. They have also 'travelled' well, as anglers have found them to be effective on lakes as diverse as Chew, Rutland and Bewl. I have even caught fish on a Connemara Black on a small stillwater in France.

But the greatest strength of the Connemara Black is as part of a team of flies for lock style drifting, and here it is without peer. In a good wave – and the Irish call anything up to a 5ft swell a 'good wave,'– it can be truly deadly. It also fishes well in our more predictable ripples and I always fish it in the middle dropper position in a team of three flies. It can occasionally be used in the bob fly position, but I find it works best in the middle, where it has just that bit more depth.

The strength of the pattern must lie in its predominantly black colouring, which suggests the confused outline of so many insects, both aquatic and terrestrial. As one of the classic winged 'wets' it has that wonderful shape that seems to be so attractive to the fish, with a combination of a swept-back wing and the bulky seal's fur body.

You have only to look at it in the tying vice to know that the complete fly looks 'right'. It has a fish-catching quality about it that defies description.

The Connemara Black is a fly that you will need in only two sizes – 10s and 12s. As a general rule, the bigger the wave, the bigger the fly, and I would only use the smaller 12 in a very gentle ripple. It can be retrieved fast across the top or more gently at a depth of 2ft. I have even taken fish on it at Loch Leven in Scotland on a fast sinking line, bringing the trout up from the deeps on a hold-and-draw retrieve.

Full tying
Hook: Partridge Captain Hamilton wet fly, size 10 or 12
Tail: Golden pheasant tippet
Butt: Copper floss
Body: Black seal's fur, or substitute
Rib: Fine copper wire
Wing: Bronze mallard
Throat: False hackle of blue jay

DUNKELD

On the first occasion that I fished on Loch Leven in Scotland, I felt somewhat over-awed by the place. The vastness of the loch, with all its islands and hidden bays, left me with a feeling of almost hopelessness. Then a trip to the local tackle shop changed all that: it wasn't too complicated they said, just head out from St Serfs and fish at least two Dunkelds on the cast.

It sounded too simple, but without any other more positive advice I did exactly that – and caught four lovely fish in an otherwise dour morning. My fellow team members had been elsewhere, using other tactics and flies, but my boat partner and I had taken seven fish between us, all of them coming to the Dunkeld. They were the only seven fish taken, in the team of six rods.

The story is told only to underline the great effectiveness of the Dunkeld. It is one of the truly great traditional wet-fly patterns of all time. It is also a fly that has far outgrown its Scottish origins, gaining universal acceptance among fly fishers all over Britain.

For me, the Dunkeld is very much a summer fly with particular relevance to the brighter, sunny days. It works best when the sun is dancing on the tinsel body, bringing out the real colour in the pattern. That combination of red and gold, with the Jungle Cock cheek (if you can get the feathers), works so well – as we say in Bristol, it is a fly that says 'hello' to the fish. I also like to use it when there is a little colour in the water, either from the green algae or from mud suspension after a good wind. On places like Grafham, where the water is almost always pretty green, the Dunkeld shines out and will always pull the fish.

Like most of the traditional wet patterns, the Dunkeld is best fished as part of a team of flies, usually taking the top or middle dropper position on the cast. However, a larger version of the fly (size 10 or even size 8) will sometimes perform as a tail fly, particularly if there are some fish fry about.

The Dunkeld can be retrieved in a variety of ways, from a slow figure-of-eight to a fast strip through the surface. The classic dibbling process, holding the flies under the rod tip at the end of the retrieve, was almost invented for patterns like this, and takes will frequently come just at the point of lift-off.

Surprisingly for such a successful fly, the Dunkeld has been little copied or varied over the years, which in itself is testimony to the effectiveness of the original. There are one or two variants, but the tying that I use is as follows:

Full tying

Hook: Partridge Captain Hamilton wet fly, sizes 10, 12 and 14
Tail: Golden pheasant crest
Body: Flat gold tinsel (copper tinsel is a useful variant)
Rib: Fine gold wire (optional)
Hackle: Hot orange hackle, tied as a beard
Cheeks: Jungle cock or substitute
Wing: Rolled bronze mallard

INVICTA

The Invicta is another of those classic winged wet-fly patterns that can stand the test of time and still perform universally well on almost any water. It is a genuine classic, with proven killing ability on waters as diverse as Lough Conn in Ireland and Rutland in Leicester.

Like all the great wet flies, it is difficult initially to see why it is so special. At first glance it doesn't look like anything that lives in stillwater and neither does it have a nymph or insect shape. It cannot be called a 'natural food' pattern because it doesn't look remotely like anything the trout eats. At best it can be said to suggest the confused outline of hatching insects such as sedge or midge, but that's all.

For me, the real secret of the Invicta (and probably many other wet flies) is, in fact, its outline or silhouette. That lovely confused shape, with wings and hackle points all over the place blends so well with the soft, muted colours to form a fly that looks right: you only have to glimpse an Invicta to know that it is going to catch a fish.

It is also one of a select number of patterns that can be fished with success at any position on the cast. As part of a team of pulled flies it probably works best in the middle position, yet I know of many anglers who swear by it on the top dropper and just as many who use it on the point. For the latter, I like to scale up the size a bit and tie it on a slightly longer hook so that it becomes more of an attractor. The heavier wire gauge also tends to help with presentation, which is an added bonus. As a useful rule-of-thumb, the standard size Invicta would be on a size 12, with the top dropper position being taken by a size 14. For the point fly you can go up to 10s or even perhaps 8s in a big wave.

The fly also works in different retrieve modes, from dead slow through to a fast strip. In general terms, I use the maxim of 'the bigger the wave, the faster the retrieve', which seems to make a lot of sense. Like any theory, of course, it is always easy to disprove – some people say that they catch on an Invicta with a static retrieve in a flat calm.

Full tying

Hook: Partridge Captain Hamilton wet fly, sizes 10, 12 and 14
Tail: Golden pheasant tippet
Body: Amber seal's fur
Rib: Flat gold or oval gold tinsel
Palmer hackle: Brown/red game
Throat hackle: Blue jay
Wing: Folded or rolled wing of hen pheasant
Option: Jungle cock cheeks improve the fly – if you can get them

MALLARD AND CLARET

This is another of those wonderful patterns that defy age, fishing consistently well year after year, on every conceivable type of water. Of all the winged wet flies it is probably the best known and most fished, and is a fly that you would find in about 90 per cent of all the fly-boxes in the world.

It is an over-worked saying, but the Mallard and Claret is one fly that you cannot afford to be without. I have used it as the all-time standby for many years, fishing it in all conditions and at any point on the cast. It works best as a middle dropper, like so many traditional wets, but in the smaller sizes (14 or 16) it can be used as a bob fly. Larger sizes, in 10s or even 8s, are useful point flies, especially when the pin fry are about in May or June.

Such versatility is almost unique in a fly, yet nobody has yet come up with a satisfactory reason to explain its effectiveness. The overall shape of the fly could be said to suggest many things, from the confused outline of a hatching nymph through to a drowned adult insect. Equally, with the wing swept well back it bears more than a passing resemblance to a small fish. The reasons for its success are unimportant, of course; what really counts is the fly's performance, and this is beyond question.

I prefer to fish the Mallard and Claret in the middle of a team of three flies. The top dropper could be a small buzzer, with a Stick Fly on the point, and this would be an ideal team for the evenings. Another good team – say, for a big wind and wave day – would be a bushy Soldier Palmer on top and a heavy Pheasant Tail (to 'anchor' the cast) on the point. The variations are endless, and the truth is that all of them will have their day. The great thing about the Mallard and Claret, above all else, is that you can have complete confidence in using it, and confidence, as we all know, is one of the most important ingredients in fishing:

Full tying

Hook: Partridge Captain Hamilton wet fly , sizes 10–14
Tail: Golden pheasant tippet feathers
Body: Dark claret seal's fur or substitute
Rib: Fine gold wire
Hackle: Claret hackle, tied as a beard
Wing: Rolled bronze mallard feather

A fly from the past, the Chief Nedabeh. A scaled-down version of this pattern, adapted to international size, is currently enjoying a revival

Attractors

IT MATTERS NOT WHETHER they are known as attractors, mini-lures or whatever, the patterns listed here are a must for any fly-box. Some are 'borderline' flies as they defy categorisation. Although I have listed them as attractors, they are still slightly suggestive or even imitative. These elements can be further enhanced by the way in which they are fished, showing yet again that versatility is one of the key factors in a truly great fly.

THE CLIFTON

Many people ask me about the names of flies, and often these are almost as intriguing as the patterns themselves. Many have strange origins – who would have thought, for instance, that the essential ingredient in a Tup's Indespensible would be the fur from a ram's scrotum? Indeed, who thought of getting fur from that particular part of the ram in the first place?

Fly names often have the name of their inventor incorporated in them, or perhaps the name of the place where they were first used. In the case of the Clifton, it is somewhat different: the fly was invented on a day when the fishing was so bad that many anglers were considering jumping off the suspension bridge at Clifton – that was, until they tried this particular pattern!

The Clifton was born on a hard day at Langford in Wiltshire. It was very cold and the trout were in a foul mood, refusing to look at anything. All the attractors had been tried as had all the nymphs, but without the slightest interest. Then one of our number, Martin Cairncross, tried one of his many experimental flies and the results were incredible. It was more of a fly-tying exercise in the search for a workable cross between a Stick Fly and a Viva, two of the best flies at Langford, but the end result proved to be even better than either of those two established favourites. This is so often the case in fly-tying. It takes an inventive mind, coupled with a good deal of common sense, to create new patterns, and it is logical to try to combine major features in known and proven patterns and to turn them into something special.

The Clifton is very special indeed. It has now caught fish all over the country, and has also worked well for me as far afield as France and Belgium, when I was fishing in the European Championships. I should perhaps stress that it is very much a small stillwater fly rather than a pattern for the big reservoirs. It can occasionally catch on the big lakes, but it is supreme as a fly for the smaller fisheries, where it can be fished slow and deep.

The Clifton is best on an intermediate or on a slow sinker. It can work on a floater if it is given a lead under-body, which helps if you are fishing among the weed-beds. It must be retrieved slowly, in a series of varied pulls and tweaks, to move the marabou fibres around.

Full tying
Hook: Partridge HIA nymph hook, size 10
Butt: Two turns of fluorescent green wool, wound tight
Body: Natural peacock herl
Rib: Copper wire (optional)
Wing: Sparse pinch of black marabou, tied 'upright'
Head: Two turns of red fluorescent wool

MONTANA VARIATION

The Montana is an American pattern that won instant acclaim in Britain. This is hardly surprising since it was devised for rainbow (and other) trout in the USA, and we are, after all, fishing here for the same species. The pattern is probably one of those flies that conveniently bridges the imaginary gap between attractor and nymph categories, but it doesn't matter what you call it – it catches fish and that's what counts. The variation that I use gives a bit more life than the original and incorporates all the advantages of marabou to the full.

Full tying
Hook: Partridge HIA, size 10
Tail: Pinch of black marabou feather, tied about half the length of
       the hook shank
Body: Black marabou fibres, wrapped around the shank

Rib: Gold oval tinsel
Thorax: Fluorescent green wool over a palmered black hackle
Wing-case: Black PT fibres

The overall effect is one of a very lifelike attractor, with a superb pulsing movement in both tail and body. If you add a lead under-body, it actually improves things at the tying stage, as the extra bulk builds up the shape. It is good at almost any speed of retrieve and can even be pulled across the top on a day when the fish look like being up in the water.

The Montana works well on any water, but is especially effective on smaller lakes. It can be cast at individual cruising fish and in such circumstances it is even better than most small imitators.

PERSUADER

Many of the flies that we use have nonsensical names, while others are obscure. Some are meaningless and owe more to the fickle nature of their inventors than anything else. But many names are descriptive, like Pheasant Tail or Stick Fly, and many more are specifically called after the things that they represent. The Damsel nymph, and the Corixa are examples of the latter. But of all the names that I have known, I believe that the Persuader must be one of the most apt, because it 'persuades' the fish that it is good enough to eat.

This pattern was invented by one of the most respected figures in game angling, John Goddard, and as such it commands instant consideration. It was originally conceived as a 'nymph for all seasons', and although it does not have any specific imitative properties, it still has that marvellous general appeal that sets it apart from the rest. The colour combination is critical and has much to do with the fly's success rate for the white/red mix is a well-proven killer.

Like all the truly great patterns, the Persuader has undergone some change and development over the years, as individual anglers have made their own alterations and adjustments to suit their own particular waters. I particularly like the use of hot orange seal's fur at the thorax, although I am not so sure about the red hackle-point tail that seems to be increasingly used these days. As with so many great flies, the original still takes a lot of beating.

The Persuader should be tied in both weighted and unweighted forms for varying water conditions. In high summer I like to fish it high in the surface film, either singly on a long leader or as part of a team of three 'pulling' flies. In both early and late season it can be best used weighted to get it down to the feeding depths. In these cases, I prefer to use either intermediate or even fast-sinking lines, and to retrieve the fly quite quickly. The pattern is even good in the middle of winter, again on the intermediate line, when the nice 'nymphy' shape seems to pick out the better fish.

Tying variations are many, with the best options including a 'wing-case' of pheasant tail fibres or a false hackle of partridge fibres.

Basic tying

Hook: Partridge emerger/nymph hook, size 10
               Or Partridge Code JIA, sizes 10–12 (for the weighted versions)
Body: White ostrich feather (or white chenille)
Rib: Silver wire or silver oval tinsel
Thorax: Hot orange seal's fur or substitute
Wing-case   Pheasant tail fibres (optional)
False hackle: Hot orange hackle fibres, tied as a beard

WOOD DUCK MUDDLER

With some of my chosen patterns we have looked at flies that are not in any way new, but are simply variations on a theme. Some base patterns are so good that many anglers copy them, often adding a little variation of their own, thereby creating a 'new' pattern. The Pheasant Tail nymph is a classic illustration of this, as is the Wood Duck Muddler.

Muddler Minnows, or simply 'Muddlers' for short, have been with us for many years, and are an established stillwater favourite. They come in all shapes and sizes, from tiny little 14s to be used on the top dropper through to huge long shank 8s or even 6s. They belong to a group of patterns that defy categorisation – that is, they are neither lure nor imitative fly, nor are they suggestive or attractor. Rather they are a unique blend of all these things, wherein lies their true worth.

The Wood Duck version of the mini-muddler is one of my favourite variations. It is intended as a boat fly, working best as top dropper on a team of loch style flies. It can sometimes work from the bank, but not nearly as effectively as when fishing the drift on a big water like Grafham or Rutland.

It first came into being when I was introduced to the marvellous barred wood duck feathers by Perk Perkins of the Orvis Company some ten years ago. These feathers have a stiking barred black-and-white pattern to them, far more so than the more conventional teal, and I immediately tied up some of the traditional wet-fly patterns that normally call for teal in the tying. The results were very effective, particularly on flies like Teal Blue and Silver, and the Peter Ross. It was then only a matter of time before I progressed to using them for these mini-muddlers.

This is a classic boat fly, and never more so than when there is a bright sun shining. Essentially, it is a bright fly, with a striking contrast in colours in its make-up, and it clearly proves that age-old saying about 'bright day, bright fly'. It should be fished fast and preferably right on the top to bring out the best of the muddler characteristics.

Full tying

Hook: Partridge Captain Hamilton wet fly, sizes 10–12
Tail: Golden pheasant crest (optional)
Body: Flat silver tinsel
Rib: Fine silver wire

Wing: Rolled wood duck feather
Head: Deer hair, clipped short. For added effect on brighter days, white dyed deer hair can be used

SIMPLE BLACK ATTRACTOR

A few years ago I described one of these 'new family' flies as part of an article designed to encourage new people to the wonders of fly-tying. The point was made then that not all fly-tying is complex, nor does it require any special manual dexterity – some of the best patterns are the simplest. The Simple Black Attractor proves this point to the full, as it uses nothing more than a hook and two pieces of tying material. It is a development from a fly that gave me huge success in 1990, and in fact took me through the National Final at Bewl in September. This variation has been used during 1990–1 winter's fishing at Langford, and the level of success convinced me that it would work all through the season; it more than justified my confidence.

Full tying
Hook: Captain Hamilton wet fly, size 10, or Scorpion wet fly, size 10
Body: None (bare hook shank)
Wing: Pinch of black marabou, tied in three-quarters of the way up the shank, and wrapping around the shank
Head: Fibres of fluorescent red marabou, wrapped around the head

WHITE BOOBY

The booby is a fundamentally different fly, developed some years ago for a very specific set of angling circumstances. Most people trace its origins back to Queen Mother Reservoir at Datchet, where they needed a fly to fish right along the bottom of the concrete banks, without snagging and without fouling in the weed. The booby was the answer and now the name refers to a whole family of patterns, each tied on the same principle and for the same mode of fishing. The trick is to use a very fast sinking line, coupled with a very short leader. The nylon can be as short as 18in or as long as 6–7ft – it depends on contour and weed growth in your chosen venue. The line is cast out and allowed to sink completely before commencing the retrieve. In this way, the line is lying right on the bottom, but the ultra-buoyant fly is suspended above. Even the slightest pull on the line transmits itself to the fly, which can thus be retrieved just above the lake-bed.

In practice, it works even better than it sounds and this method has accounted for many fish in recent years. A very heavy line must be used for it all to work properly – slow to medium sinkers don't have the density to pull down the fly. Some anglers even use two boobys at a time, one tied very short and the other at around 5–6ft. This has the effect of exploring a greater area and can pull fish that are feeding at lesser depths.

The booby comes in all colours and you can experiment to find those best for your local water. However, the basic tying principles are the same throughout, and although it looks complex initially, they are actually quite simple to tie:

Full tying

Hook: Captain Hamilton wet fly, size 10

Tail: Tag of green fluorescent wool (optional)

Body: Green fluorescent wool

Wing: Pinch of white marabou feather, tied just beyond the bend

Head: Ethafoam balls, tied in either side of the head. You may find that it helps to enclose them in a piece of nylon mesh (discarded tights), or as an alternative you can cut one complete piece of foam in a figure-of-eight shape and tie this in on top of the shank. The size of the head must be big enough to let the fly float freely: test it by throwing it hard onto the surface of the bath-water or sink.

The Dries

THIS IS UNDOUBTEDLY THE area of greatest innovation in fly-tying and probably the one where most work is still to be done. Every season sees a new interpretation of

established patterns; even within a developing sport, it is very much a growth area.

These following dries have filled my box for the last five years and they have been responsible for a substantial number of fish. The list does not pretend to be exhaustive, but it does account for by far the greatest bulk of my stillwater dry flyfishing.

Adult red midge

AMBER OR CLARET HOPPERS

By late spring or early summer, days of cold winds and chilled fingers are definitely a thing of the past. On most fisheries it is a case of floating lines, smaller flies and some genuinely imitative fishing. The big black lures of early season are just a fading memory.

High up on everyone's list of imitative flies must come some of the 'new generation' dry-fly patterns. There are some highly complicated variations around, but the originals are still favourite and flies like the hoppers and Shipman's Buzzers are now almost household names. Indeed, I would be perfectly happy to fish a hopper and a Shipman's on an exclusive basis, virtually throughout the year.

Further, if I had to specify just two colours for the hopper they would certainly be amber and claret. The hopper probably accounts for something in the region of 40 per cent of all the fish I catch on dry fly, and claret and amber have been in pole position in my fly-box for the last three seasons. The Claret Hopper is best as point fly in the team, although it can be used in the smaller sizes (12s and 14s) on the dropper, particularly in a good wave. But the best hook size by far is a 10, where the extra weight in the hook gives the added benefit of better turnover on the cast and consequently better presentation. Tying details for the claret version are shown here; for the amber version the only change is the seal's fur.

Tying the Claret Hopper is very straightforward and there is no mystique in tying any of the dry-fly patterns. This myth was put about by one or two tyers who had a vested interest in making it sound more complicated than it really is. No special skills are needed and any average tyer will be able to produce a perfectly acceptable hopper.

Place the hook in the vice and lay a good base of claret tying silk. There is no tail, so first tie in the rib; this can be either fine gold wire or fine pearly tinsel, which is a great variation for brighter, sunny days. Then take a pinch of claret seal's fur (or substitute) and form a level body up to about ⅛in behind the head. Make about five or six turns of rib.

The legs are formed from knotted individual fibres of pheasant tail, and the knots should be made about ¼–⅓in from the points. This can be a fiddly process and if you have poor eyesight, you may need some help.

Tie in the legs, three on each side, pointing back and down. Too many patterns have the legs pointing in all directions, which is wrong. They should trail back and down, helping the fly to sit nicely down in the water.

Finally, tie in about three turns of red game hackle at the head, tie off and varnish. At this stage, I like to give all my hoppers an initial application of Gink at the tying bench. This makes them really waterproof as the Gink has plenty of time to work well into the fly before it is used. A very light application of Gink at the waterside is all that is then needed.

Apart from the rib, the only other variation is to use claret-dyed pheasant tail fibres and a claret hackle, which can give a better overall effect to the fly and may help to fool the really fussy fish.

Full tying

Hook: Partridge Captain Hamilton, size 10, or Kamasam B400, size 10
Body: Claret seal's fur or substitute. Amber Hopper uses a mix of fiery
          brown/amber fur.
Rib: Fine gold wire or fine pearly tinsel
Legs: Knotted pheasant tail fibres (6). Natural for Amber Hopper, claret-dyed
          for claret version
Hackle: Red game

DRY BIBIO

It is often said that the current craze on stillwaters of fishing 'the dries' is only in its infancy. It is such a recent phenomenon that there is still much to be done in terms of fly development. Already, new flies are being developed. Existing flies are being modified and varied, and the more we learn from experience the faster this development will take place. In the field of competitions, in particular, there are some inventive minds at work. It was the result of a conversation between two competitors that led to the creation of the Dry Bibio.

We had been fishing Chew for several days and the fish were well up and feeding right on the top. Black Hoppers were working, but we felt that we were not getting nearly as many takes as we should have had, especially in view of the huge numbers of trout that were moving. Autopsies showed that there were a lot of small black beetles in the diet, many of which had a red sheen to them. They were also much smaller than our hoppers, so out of desperation we decided to Gink up a normal Bibio. The result was instant: the fish devoured the fly, even though it was sinking too often because of the heavy hook.

After that day, it was a simple matter to make some slight modifications to the pattern and to produce the Dry Bibio. A lightweight hook pattern is essential, and the Partridge code L3A Captain Hamilton dry fly is perfect. Size 12 is best, but we have also found size 14 to be useful on calm days. The variations are a well picked-out seal's fur body and a stiff but short palmered hackle. Essentially, the fly looks like a 'hairy' version of the normal Bibio.

Full tying
Hook: Partridge Code L3A, size 12–14
Body: Black seal's fur or substitute. Small pinch of red seal's fur in centre body
Rib: Fine silver wire
Hackle: Stiff black cock hackle, palmered

Note: Seal's fur well picked out, either with dubbing needle or Velcro pad

SHIPMAN'S BUZZER

Within the circles of competitive flyfishing, several names stand out as major achievers – anglers of special note who can be consistently relied upon to produce fish, even in seemingly impossible conditions. Among this select band is an even higher echelon, made up of anglers who have made a lasting impression on the sport, either by outstanding success or by inventing a fundamentally new tactic or fly pattern. Dave Shipman from Whittlesey is such a man.

As recently as five years ago, the use of dry fly on stillwaters was virtually unheard of. Then we began to hear rumours of a fundamentally new fly that was being used to great effect on the Midlands waters of Rutland and Grafham, a new style of buzzer that was designed to sit on top of the water and to be fished 'dry'. It was being called loosely after its inventor, and in the space of less than a season it had established itself as a genuinely 'vital' pattern: the Shipman's Buzzer.

These were the pioneering days of the dry fly, and Dave frequently managed to come in with a lovely bagful of residential rainbows taken on his buzzer, while lesser mortals were still struggling to achieve anything with the stockies and wet flies. Even in that first year, one of the most striking aspects of dry fly was that it could be proved to single out the better fish, those that had become used to seeing lures and nymphs and had become fussy and selective.

In five short years the Shipman's Buzzers (it is not just a single fly, but a title for a whole range of variations) have been refined and developed. They now form the

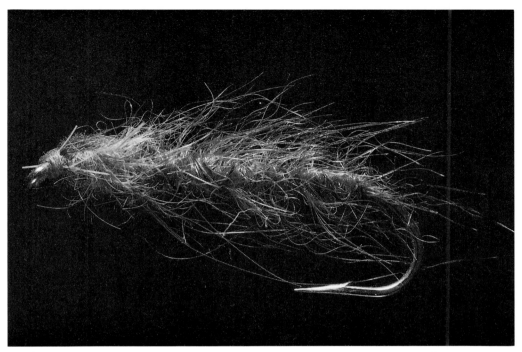

On most dries, the dubbing is well picked out. This provides a better silhouette, and is far more attractive when viewed in the surface film

The Green Emerger, one of the classic stillwater dry fly styles. The colour is almost irrelevant; it is the shape and silhouette that really matter

backbone of any dry-fly selection and still account for about 30 per cent of the fish I take on dries throughout the year. Despite the huge number of variations, the original is still the best, although it is now used in a host of different colours. The seal's fur blends of reds, hot orange and fiery brown are favourite, but claret is also good, as are the browns and olives for the evenings.

Full tying

Hook:	Partridge Captain Hamilton, sizes 10–16, or Kamasan B170
Tail:	White wool or white floss. Some even tie in white hackle points
Body:	Blended seal's fur
Rib:	Silver or pearly tinsel
Forward breathers:	White wool or alternatives

As the tying details suggest, this fly could not be simpler to tie; it can be mastered by even the novice tyer. The original fly contained a bulky seal's fur application, but recently I have been tying them very sparsely, experimenting with much finer ribbing. A fine copper tinsel works well with the red and brown furs, and fine pearly is brilliant with the claret.

As seal's fur becomes progressively difficult to obtain, the new micro chenille dubbing from Veniard is an ideal substitute and is even easier to tie.

Shipman's Buzzers are designed to sit right in the surface film and should be fished static. a light application of Gink is needed and the fly sits well on the water due to the balancing effect of the wool at fore and aft. It can be fished in all conditions from flat calm to big wave, but is absolutely deadly in the evening rise when the darker colours are best. On Grafham, where there is often some heavy colour in the water, the brighter reds are preferred and fish will frequently come for them from nowhere, without any warning.

WINGED EMERGER

Most readers will know by now that there is no mystery about 'the dries'. Hopefully, I have illustrated how easy it is to fish them, and also that most of the patterns are straightforward to tie. The Winged Emerger is no exception, and together with the immortal hopper it ranks as a favourite dry.

At this stage it is important to understand the actual fishing role of the fly in order to tie it correctly. Emergers are designed loosely to represent insects – mostly midge or sedge – as they emerge from the pupal shuck at the water surface. The outline is the crucial factor here, far more so than the colour. The fish will see a fairly confused silhouette of trailing legs, wing-cases and body; in anything but a flat calm it will only have a few seconds to decide whether it is food or not, and provided the shape looks right it will take. Size and colour are important, but not nearly as much as outline.

Consequently, the tyer must always think about how the emerger sits in the surface film and take an imaginary trout's-eye view of the fly, which is from beneath. Many anglers look at the fly in the vice (from the side) and doubt its worth. But if they took a moment to look at it from beneath they would begin to see its real value.

For most of the time I like to clip a pair of scissors across the underside of the hackle, which helps the fly to sit nicely down in the water. Remember, we are imitating something that is struggling through the water surface as opposed to sitting on it. The clipped hackle is great in this respect and further improves presentation as the fly invariably lands the right way up.

Full tying

Hook: Partridge Captain Hamilton dry fly, size 12 or 14
            Or Kamasan B400, size 12 or 14
Body: Seal's fur or substitute (Veniard Easy Dub micro chenille is an
            ideal substitute)
Rib: Very fine copper/gold wire
Wing: White hackle points
Hackle: Red game (clipped on the underside)

Tying procedures are quite simple. Keep the body slim, but pick out some fibres with either a dubbing needle or a small Velcro pad. The best colours for emergers are claret, red or amber, although on occasions you will need to match the hatch with greens and ginger. They are such good flies that you can never have enough of them in the box.

On really fussy days, for instance in a flat calm when the fish are being totally selective, try a single Winged Emerger on a 12ft leader – it can be deadly.

DRY OLIVE

This little fly is a departure from the 'usual' emerger as it is designed to sit right up on the surface – most emerger patterns are supposed to sit *in*, rather than *on* the surface film. However, I would not suggest that this fly is in any way a close copy pattern, because it is still more of a suggestive than a direct imitator. It was designed for those days when the fish are up on the top and feeding, but also when there is a good wind and wave that makes life harder when fishing 'normal' emergers.

The problems in a big wind are twofold: first, you cannot see your flies very well, and second, they tend to get waterlogged and become submerged much more quickly, thereby negating many of their benefits. The Dry Olive has a stiff hackle and a very spiky profile, which makes it sit up well on the top. When properly Ginked it is a hard fly to sink, maintaining its buoyancy for a long time before a re-Gink is necessary. With the gold hook it is also very visible, another advantage when fishing in a big wave. This gold effect combines with the hackle colour to form an overall olive colour that is close to most of the natural stillwater olives that occur on our lakes, and it also makes a fair suggestion of the adult green midges that tumble along the surface in a good blow.

Like most dry flies, the Dry Olive is best fished static, cast into the path of a cruising fish or simply left on the top until a take occurs. In practice this is not so easy in a big wave and a fair amount of recasting will be required. On odd occasions, the fish will take this fly 'pulled' as it naturally creates a wake, but for most of the time it is best left static.

Full tying

Hook: Partridge dry-fly hook, sizes 12–14, or fine wire gold hook (if you can find one)

Tail: Pinch of olive hackle fibres

Body: Flat gold tinsel or flat pearly tinsel over a base of gold

Rib: Fine gold wire (through the palmer hackle)

Hackle: Stiff olive cock

CLARET RAIDER

It was Bristol's John Horsey who first introduced me to the Claret Raider a few years ago. John has been at the forefront of stillwater dry-fly development, much of it taking place on Chew Valley – probably the ultimate top-of-the-water fishery in the country, and certainly one of the best for fishing 'the dries'.

Indeed, most of us in the Bristol Reservoirs FFA team have been instrumental in developing dry patterns, having learned the original concept from friends such as Bob Worts and Dave Shipman in the Midlands. Fly development has been fast and furious over the last five years, and the angling world as a whole owes a great debt to the pioneering few.

The raider is one of the general suggestive dry flies: in other words, it loosely suggests items on the trout's menu, as opposed to actually representing a particular item. In some ways it is like a simplified emerger, but without any hackle or false wing. It is a simple fly to tie, requiring a minimum of material and no special tying skills.

As with most stillwater dries, the raider is best used in conjunction with other patterns, as part of a team. I find that it works well on either the top or middle dropper positions, perhaps alternating with a Shipman's Buzzer. A larger dry such as a hopper will usually take the point fly position, thus ensuring good balance and leader turnover. On really fussy days, and particularly in a flat calm, the Claret Raider can be used as a single fly on a longer leader, to guarantee perfect presentation.

When tying, make sure that the rear part of the body is tied slim, with a minimum of seal's fur. Then build up the thorax to a reasonable bulk and remember to pick out the fibres on top of the completed fly. This helps it to sit well down in the water surface, as well as enhancing the overall silhouette of the fly. It is almost worth running the scissors under the finished thorax, to clear any unwanted fibres.

Full tying

Hook: Partridge Captain Hamilton dry fly, sizes 12 and 14

Rear body: Claret seal's fur or substitute, tied slim

Rib: Three or four turns of pearly tinsel (a good alternative is fine silver wire)

Thorax: Claret seal's fur, tied bulky. Picked out fibres on top of the fly

SHUCK FLY

A fly pattern is not a fly when it represents a shuck rather than the fly itself. This needs to be said at the outset, because the Shuck Fly looks like nothing you will have seen before and does not conform to our 'normal' understanding of artificial fly patterns. It does, however, catch a lot of fish, and in the summer months it can have its day, even when absolutely nothing else works.

The thinking behind this pattern is very simple. Often you will be on the water with literally hundreds of fish moving around you, all of which refuse to take any offerings. They will be rising freely, with the classic head-and-tail rise of surface-feeding fish, but all conventional flies are steadfastly ignored. At such times the fish may well be 'shucking', mopping up the midge or sedge cases that lie flat on the surface.

This may seem like a fairly fruitless activity on the part of the fish, as the nutritional value of empty cases is somewhat questionable, but the fact is that they do it. They also become preoccupied with the shuck as a food item, ignoring even large natural adult insects in the process. No pupa imitation will tempt them, nor will the best-tied dry fly. The angler is therefore left with only one option – to imitate the shuck.

In fact, there is an alternative option, to retire to the pub, a course of action favoured by many and with much to commend it! However, those of us made of sterner stuff will persevere, and the rewards can be great. The Shuck Fly illustrated here is my best pattern so far and it has caught fish for over three seasons in the conditions described above. It has to be fished in the surface film, just as you would with a more conventional dry fly, and it must be kept absolutely static. Because of the nature of this feeding pattern, conditions are generally calm or near-calm, which makes it easy to see the fly on the surface. Takes are almost always very confident, and no big strike is called for, just a slow tightening on the line.

Never be tempted to fish the Shuck Fly as part of a team, unless you fish two of them at once. It is far better to fish it as a single fly, on a relatively long leader of 12–15ft. As with all dry-fly or surface fishing, the leader itself must be well treated to sink, or you will spoil the presentation.

Full tying

Hook: Partridge Captain Hamilton wet fly, sizes 12–14
Tail wisps: Cream seal's fur, tied very straggly
Body: A half-inch piece of Ethafoam, cut to shape, and caught in at the tail by a
             few turns of tying silk
             Remainder of hook shank left bare

Nymphs

THERE MUST BE AS many nymph patterns as there are natural species, and any shortlist must be regarded as the absolute minimum for the fly-box. Similarly, there are many local variations in colour and shape on most of the prime insect orders, and a sedge pupa, for instance, can be a very different insect in different waters. Local observation, and at least a superficial study of the

Freshwater shrimp

insect life on the water you intend to fish, will hold the key. The advantage about the following list is that all the patterns are proven, on a variety of waters and in a huge variation of conditions.

GREEN TAG STICK

While I would never claim to have invented any particular fly pattern, I certainly do take the credit for popularising this particular fly. The Green Tag Stick, or GTS for short, is one of my all-time favourite patterns. So good is this fly that I would, without hesitation, rank it as one of the top five stillwater patterns. Some flies fall in and out of favour with anglers, while others are more 'one-day wonders' than anything else. Some are little more than figments of some writer's imagination, and there are even some that are promoted as being real catchers simply to sell more flies – the ugly head of commercialism raises itself all too readily in fly fishing. For the most part, anglers are aware of such confidence tricks, and they can quickly see through any blatant hypes. Equally, most anglers know a good thing when they see it, and there can be few fly-boxes in the land that do not contain some Green Tag Sticks in varying sizes.

The great advantage of the GTS is that it really looks as though it is going to catch fish. It has that marvellous nymph-based shape, coupled with those essential ingredients of colour and movement. Even more, it has a kind of insect quality about it, or the look of a fly that is going to suggest or represent a whole variety of things in the water. In this respect, appearances are about right because the GTS was indeed designed to look like many trout food items. The original concept was a fly that loosely represented the caddis or sedge pupa. This it does admirably, but it doesn't stop there. When fished fast it hints at damsel nymph or even small fish fry. When fished slow, trundled along the bottom on a slow sink line, it looks like many of the creatures that live on the bottom.

Even this is not the whole story, however, because the truth is that it is a pattern that will catch fish in all conditions of wind and weather, on all waters large and small, and at all depths. I use it as a single fly for Avington or Damerham, yet I am just as happy to use it as point fly in a team of three on Chew or Rutland – it really is that versatile.

The GTS can and should be tied in both weighted and unweighted versions. For most of the time I prefer it on a good medium-wire nymph hook, like the Partridge H1A, but it can also be effective on a standard shank, heavy-wire hook like the J1A. As a final comment on its versatility, you will need it in all sizes from 10 down to 14.

Full tying
Hook: Partridge nymph hook, code H1A
Tail: Butt of fluorescent green wool (two or three tight turns
           around the bend)
Body: Natural peacock herl
Rib: Copper wire or oval gold tinsel
Hackle: Soft hen badger hackle (three turns). Really soft and
           relatively long-fibred hackles can impart extra life.
           For a more sombre fly, substitute a dark red
           game hen hackle

BUZZERS

There are few, if any, stillwaters in the land that do not contain midge pupae to a greater or lesser degree, and there should not be any fly-boxes that do not contain some of the finest pupae imitations – the humble buzzers. Like the natural insects buzzers come in all shapes, sizes and colours, and a little local study will point you at the best combination for your home water. Beyond that, however, there is a pattern that has served me well for so many years that it cannot be excluded in this list. It has caught fish in the Mendips, yet it has also taken them from the mountain lakes of New Zealand, which must be the ultimate in versatility.

This fly fishes at any position on the cast, although it is probably best on the top and middle dropper spots. In the daytime I would fish two of them with a Stick Fly on the point to anchor things down, but in the evening rise I would simply put up a full team of three.

The little fluorescent wool collar is a key factor in the fly's appeal, and this can be changed for either green or peach on occasions. Even so, red is much the best colour all round, and this supremacy has been proven after many years of experimentation. Indeed, it will be seen quickly that this is a pattern that just begs for variations, and I wish you luck with any that you try.

Full tying
Hook: Captain Hamilton wet fly, or Kamasan B170, sizes 10–16
Tail: Wisp of white wool to stimulate breathers
Body: Black floss or seal's fur
Rib: Fine gold wire
Thorax butt: One turn of fluorescent red wool
Thorax: Peacock herl
Wine-case: PT fibres
Breather: Wisp of white wool

OMBUDSMAN

I first became aware of the Ombudsman when I read Brian Clarke's book *The Pursuit of Stillwater Trout*. Like everything else in that book, it had a ring of common sense about it, and it looked like the sort of fly that ought to catch fish. Some flies have that kind of natural life to them, a certain quality that sets them apart from the rest, and they have something in their overall appearance that builds your confidence as an angler. The Ombudsman is such a fly.

Although it looks very 'insecty', the Ombudsman is not a specific representation of any particular food item. Rather, it is one of the best of the general suggestive patterns, that group of flies that includes such all-time favourites as the Stick Fly and the Pheasant Tail. They look roughly like a host of insects from sedge pupae to large midge, with even a hint of damsel nymph about them. As such, they have a good all-round appeal, and are the first choice on a day when nothing is showing and there is no fly life around to give you a clue as to what fly to put on.

Without doubt, the Ombudsman is best as a weighted nymph and you should build up a level under body of lead wire on the hook shank before tying the fly itself. It can be used in a non-weighted form, but I have not found it to be nearly so effective. It is supreme as a deep water nymph, either fished at some speed across the bottom or just inched around among the weed-beds. It is great for the smaller stillwaters, particularly in the smaller sizes.

Another huge benefit is that it is one of the very few flies that are good for the whole season. I use it in larger sizes in April and May on sinking lines, moving through to 12s and 14s on a floater for the summer months. At the end of the season you can then move up to the larger sizes again, especially when there are any sedges around.

Full tying
Hook: Partridge nymph hook, code H1A, sizes 8, 10, 12 and 14 depending on the season
Body: Natural peacock herl
Rib: Oval gold tinsel
Wing: 'Rolled' wing of turkey or substitute
Hackle: Two turns of badger
    An underbody of lead wire is virtually compulsory

GRENADIER

The Grenadier is one of the classic enigmas of flyfishing. Its origins are already shrouded in the mists of time; it is a mix of traditional, imitative and close-copy patterns, and it will catch fish when all else fails. It is a fly that has been copied, altered and tied in a hundred variants, but always fishermen revert to the original pattern – the infamous Grenadier.

The Grenadier is a pattern devised and developed on the shores of Blagdon between the wars by the great stillwater angler Dr Bell. His pioneering work in terms of investigative fly dressing is well known, and he is universally acknowledged as being one of the original innovators of close-copy patterns. But for all that – and here is the enigma – it is unclear what he was copying when he created the Grenadier. In general shape and outline, it is reminiscent of many of the traditional spider-type dressings and belongs to an era when wet flies were very much the vogue on both river and lock. However, if it was designed to represent a particular species, we shall never know exactly which one, as there are no records. Despite delving deep into the Blagdon archives, there is no cast-iron proof what Dr Bell was imitating.

Some people may say that the motive matters little and what really counts is the effectiveness of the fly, which is undeniable. It is also fairly certain that the field can be considerably narrowed, because the large red midge that predominate on Chew and Blagdon must have figured strongly in the early stages. These chironomids, almost half an inch long in the pupa stage, are a main feature of the Bristol waters from late May onwards. They can hatch in such profusion that fish become totally preoccupied with them, to the exclusion of everything else, and they have the added benefit of being day-hatching flies as opposed to evening flies only.

Nowadays, the Grenadier has far outgrown its Bristol origins. It has been copied and varied, but seldom bettered and the fly that I use today is little changed from Bell's original. The body needs to be fairly slim and a softer hackle is advisable as it imparts more life. Some of the best variations will substitute a dark coachman, badger, or even a hot orange hackle to good effect.

Full tying
Hook: Partridge G3A or, on rougher days, Kamasan B175, sizes 10–14
Body: Hot orange scarlet seal's fur blend
Rib: Four turns of oval gold tinsel
Hackle: Two or three turns or furnace

THE SILVER PHEASANT TAIL

Most trout-fishing lakes have some coarse fish in them, and it is the fry of these fish that hold the secret of the Silver Pheasant Tail. This is a cross between an imitative pattern and a general suggestive one, that elusive combination. It works well in early summer when the coarse fish fry are barely an inch long, and it seems to work just as well in the later months of the year, by which time those same fry can be anything up to 2in in length.

The Pheasant Tail is one of the most copied and varied of all stillwater fly patterns. You can experiment with different coloured thorax materials, as well as varying the colour of the pheasant tail fibres themselves, thanks to the now widely available dyed tails. Some of these variations are new, but the Silver PT is an established favourite.

I first started using this pattern about ten years ago, and it is so good that I would rate it unquestionably in my top ten stillwater patterns. It is best fished on a standard shank size 10 hook and should be the point fly in any team. It can be weighted for probing deeper water, or it can be tied on a lightweight hook for fishing right in the surface. It is a classic 'pulling' fly for the boat, yet it is also a super pattern for slow prospecting along the bank. As you can see, it is very much one of those special flies that qualifies for the term 'all-rounder'.

I like to have this fly in my box in a whole range of hook sizes and wire. As the ultimate point fly, it would be tied on the heavier wire J1A hook in size 10, but it also works as a mid-season dropper pattern on the slightly lighter emerger hooks, in either 12s or 14s. I think that its appeal must be the coupling of the overall nymph shape with that discreet flash of silver at the thorax to enhance the 'life' in the fly.

Full tying
Hook: Partridge, code J1A, or Living Nymph, sizes 10–14
Tail: Pinch of badger hackle fibres
Body: Natural PT fibres
Rib: Fine silver wire
Thorax: Flat silver tinsel
Covers: PT fibres
Throat: Pinch of badger hackle fibres, tied as a false hackle

AMBER NYMPH

The Amber Nymph is one of those patterns that has about as many variations as there are fishermen. Like the Pheasant Tail or the buzzer, there are countless variations on the same theme, and every fly fisherman has his own version. One of the reasons for this is that the Amber Nymph is a close-copy pattern as it represents the nymph stage of one of the most prolific stillwater insects, the sedge. With so many variations in the colour, shape and size of the natural insects, it follows that anglers will adapt the original pattern to their own waters, matching their particular local species.

The other reason for all these variations is that all tyers love to try to develop and improve a good fly pattern, and the Amber Nymph is definitely a very good pattern. My own favourite sticks fairly closely to John Goddard's original but with a fundamental change in the blended seal's fur thorax. By now, readers will know that I rarely, if ever, use seal's fur in one colour as I prefer to blend two or more colours together to give a better overall appearance. On Chew and Blagdon, the colour of the natural sedges is very close to those on the original Amber Nymph, but the thorax needs to be blended to get that amber/ginger/red colouring.

This fly has caught well for me on almost every major stillwater in the country. It was a big help in winning the 1987 national at Draycote, but has subsequently done very well on Grafham, Rutland and Bewl. I like to fish it very slowly, on a floating line, and right up in the water surface. For bank fishing it is good as a point fly, but on boats I would rather see it on the top dropper. A slow retrieve is best, with a steady figure-of-eight being the most effective.

There is also a green version that works well in late summer; for this you will simply need to substitute the 'red' thorax with a 50/50 blend of bottle-green and dark olive fur. On some of the high level moorland reservoirs in the South West I even have a black version, to match up with the many black terrestrial insects that get blown onto the water.

Full tying
Hook: Partridge, code J1A, sizes 10, 12 and 14
Rear body: Cream/light amber seal's fur blend
Rib: Fine gold wire
Thorax: Equal blend of orange, amber/ginger seal's fur
Covers: Pheasant tail fibres
False hackle: Red game hackle – just a pinch tied as a beard

DIAWL BACH

It is often said that the simplest things in life are the best, and this is also true of fly patterns. Some of the most successful flies of all time consist of little more than one or two pieces of material and a hook. Sparse they may be, but still there is a shape, an outline or an overall 'look' to the fly that is irresistible. The Diawl Bach is such a pattern.

The Diawl Bach is probably one of the oldest flies in my box and it has featured in the 'essential' category for almost thirty years. It was introduced to me by a doyen of Bristol angling, the late Stan Pope, although its origins, as the name implies, are from the other side of the Severn Bridge.

Although it is by no means a close-copy pattern, the Diawl Back most certainly does have more than a passing resemblance to both midge and sedge pupae, and thus it falls very firmly into the suggestive category. I prefer to fish it just sub-surface, always on a floating line, and in either the top or middle dropper positions. In any kind of a hatch it is viable, and in the evenings it is virtually compulsory. Perhaps its greatest strength, though, is as a fly for those daytime hatches, when the fish are being overly selective and ignoring the more elaborate buzzer patterns. In clear water, its drab colouring raises no alarm signals and it is invariably taken with confidence.

I like to have the Diawl Bach in a range of sizes, but the most useful are 12s and 14s. The larger fly works best in the evening, when a 10 can also be helpful, particularly if there is still a good ripple.

One great advantage of this pattern is that it is very easy to tie. Even the worst tyer in the world could make an acceptable Diawl Bach and fish it with the fullest confidence.

Full tying
Hook: Partridge, code E1A, or Kamasan B170, sizes 10, 12 and 14
Tail: A few strands of brown hackle fibres
Body: Two strands of peacock herl
Rib: Fine gold wire (optional)
Throat: A few strands of brown hackle fibres, tied as a beard, swept well back

The Diawl Bach, one of the best imitative/suggestive nymph patterns

EPILOGUE

In many ways, this book is an explanation of my philosophy on flyfishing. What happens with rod and line is important, but of even greater relevance is the feeling that an angler has for his sport and his empathy with the fishing environment. Truly advanced flyfishing transcends the clinical elements of tackle, tactics and technique. These things are vital, certainly, but of equal importance is the angler's affinity with his surroundings: without an appreciation of the countryside, and the wealth of bird, animal and plant life that it contains, any fisherman becomes little more than an intruder. It may seem a paradox to some, but all country sportsmen are essentially conservationists. If it were not for sporting guns, then the pheasant, grouse and partridge would be rarities in Britain, and the pastel Christmas card scenes would be a myth. In the same vein, many of our rivers and lakes would be devoid of life without anglers, at best providing facilities for water-skiers or yachtsmen. At worst, and as many are on the Continent, they would be polluted shells, with no life other than bubbling gas and evil bacteria. Because of the sporting fraternity, therefore, I have an inherent optimism for the future of country sports. The clamouring yet ignorant voice of the 'anti' lobby, that kill-joy element of a misguided or disruptive few, will not prevail. If it did, then the countryside as we know it would disappear, and there is a growing enlightenment to ensure that this does not happen.

Enlightenment is not enough, however, and we all have a part to play in the protection and promotion of an acceptable face of flyfishing. The sight of a large angler bludgeoning a small trout to death is an emotive one, particularly to the lay public. Just as I will not kill a fish for an angling video, neither will I take those awful photographs of piles of dead trout that are supposed to signify a 'successful' day's fishing. Catch-and-release for the camera is a good thing, and may yet be the way forward for the real protection of angling's image.

Beyond this, I firmly believe that how we fish is important. Television viewers can easily appreciate subtlety on the snooker table, precision at the dart-board, or supreme co-ordination on the ski-slopes. In the same way, top-flight anglers can and should promote excellence in flyfishing. Thus, advanced flyfishing is about a blending of the finer ethics and traditions with modern thinking and some genuine innovation. Huge advances have been made in tackle technology in recent years and the evolution of fly patterns is a continuous process. As greater numbers take up the sport, so does the pressure on fisheries increase, with the fish becoming better educated and more fussy. Tactics, flies and watercraft evolve to cope with such changes.

But through all this, one factor stays constant and that is the simple reason for actually going fishing. It is for pleasure first and foremost, and for relaxation in lovely surroundings. It is also for the challenge and perhaps the fulfilment of our latent hunting instincts. In its finest form, it is for the solitude of one man with a fly rod, pitting his ability against a wild and cunning adversary that is totally at home in its environment.

The way in which we anglers enter that environment is crucial to the ethos of this book. We should enjoy it, but leave it unmarked by our passing. We need to understand it, with all its plant and animal inhabitants, and to appreciate its fragile balance. If we can fool a fish into thinking that our creations of fur and feather are good enough to eat, then should we not consider leaving that same fish, alive, and wiser for the experience?

Above all, I enjoy catching fish. The methods and flies used in the process are all in this book, but so too is my philosophy on fishing. A man's 'feel' for his sport is probably the hardest thing to describe, yet it is of paramount importance. Without it, all else is wasted.

Acknowledgements

IT IS A STRANGE paradox that although angling is in many ways a solitary sport, it is also one that needs to be shared with friends. Both successes and failures are either more pleasurable or poignant when aired in good company, and I count myself fortunate to have built up a long list of friendships through my flyfishing life. They are too numerous to mention individually, but to them, and to every boat partner with whom I have ever shared a day afloat, I send my thanks. Without all those shared experiences my angling memories would be so much poorer.

To many members of the angling press I am also grateful. Without the pens of hawk-eyed editors, fanatics like me tend to get too lyrical about our sport, and on many occasions they have kept me in check. Roy Westwood of *Anglers' Mail* and *Stillwater Trout Angler*; David Goodchild of *Salmon Trout & Sea Trout*; Mark Bowler of *Flyfishing & Fly Tying;* and Sandy Leventon of *Trout & Salmon*. All are now friends and have allowed some snippets to feature in this book that were originally penned for them.

Thanks are also due in no small measure to Geoff Clarkson and Mike Childs, both pillars of the Confederation of English Fly Fishers. Their support and encouragement has soothed many a competition day and they have provided a steadying hand when enthusiasm and adrenalin threatened. Goodness knows how they put up with me for all these years.

Special thanks are due to Chris Klee, Bob Handford, Ian Williamson, Kim Lucas and all the staff of Bristol Water. They are fortunate enough to manage the finest stillwaters in Britain (and probably Europe and the world) in the shape of Chew and Blagdon, where so many happy hours of research have been spent. The Bristol school of learning would not be the paragon that it is without them.

I would also like to thank Dave Grove, who is responsible for a lot of the line drawings. As well as being a highly successful angler, Dave is also a superb artist, and has made a major contribution to this and other works.

I would like to add a special word of thanks to Terry Griffiths for his superb photography. Terry is my partner in crime on the magazine *Stillwater Trout Angler*, as well as being a brilliant photographer, he is also one of the best fly tiers in the business. Also to Roy Westwood, editor of *Stillwater Trout Angler*, I extend my thanks for allowing me the use of some special photographs.

And finally to Angie, my partner and best friend in life. Her contribution to this book and to all my writings is enormous, for without her attention to fine detail I am sure it would not scan, or indeed make any sense at all.

Index